The resegregation of America:

1

Where's our Rosa Parks?

By: Dwayne D. Willis, MA, MSW

"IF YOU CAN CONVINCE THE LOWEST WHITE MAN HE'S BETTER THAN THE BEST COLORED MAN, HE WON'T NOTICE YOU'RE PICKING HIS POCKETS. HELL, GIVE HIM SOMEBODY TO LOOK DOWN ON, AND HE'LL EMPTY HIS POCKETS FOR YOU."

PRESIDENT LYNDON JOHNSON

Introduction

Way back in 1954, because of a ruling by the United States Supreme Court, schools in the United States were officially desegregated. Needless to say, there was a lot of white people who did not take this news well. There were lots of crosses burned in the south and in other areas during this time. From desegregation to forced bussing to affirmative action in order to achieve racial equality in our schools, we have toyed with all types of social and educational interventions. Some worked well, some not so much. All to create that more perfect union.

But lately there has been a recent phenomenon in which blacks and whites are starting to resegregate, attending schools with their own race and kind. The question begs to be asked, is this by design or just by occurrence? When I was doing research on this book that was the primary question I wanted to answer, but I soon discovered that this question was more complex than the simple two prong answer. Much more complex. Isn't that the way it is when human beings are involved and their social environment? I was seeking an answer with coincided with my belief that blacks had just gotten tired of all the bullshit of the white people and withdrew to be with their own group. Kind of a "strength in numbers" strategy. Or was it something akin to the old practice of "redlining" of certain neighborhoods to keep blacks out of white schools? After you read this book, you can draw your own conclusions.

Chapter One

What exactly is going on Here?

A good place to start if you want to find the root cause of a problem, no matter whether it is on the micro, mezzo, or macro level is attempt to identify the factors contributing to the problem in the first place. Since education, and by extension, resegregation is definitely a macro level issue, it stands to reason that the factors causing it would also be one the macro level as well.

First would be the growth of charter schools, many of which are highly segregated, and is the reason why some are now taking steps to become intentionally diverse. But housing patterns, experts agree, are the biggest barrier standing in the way of integrated schools. This is not only true for regular charter schools, but also the parochial counterparts. Segregated neighborhoods, due to zoning laws, racial steering, and other factors, will have segregated schools within them. It's hard to get around the facts that urban, and many suburban, neighborhoods in the U.S. are quite racially homogenous, and that children, especially the youngest ones, can't travel great distances alone to get to school. This limits the cohorts of students unless they fall into upper middle and upper class, both socially and economically. Experts largely see efforts to integrate schools doomed without integrating residential neighborhoods as well, a challenge that goes far beyond education.

Secondly, despite being among the most diverse cities in the U.S., New York City's school admission policies fortify a system of segregation, experts say. Middle schools screen students by test scores and attendance records, and black and Hispanic students are clustered in low-scoring schools plagued by attendance problems, so they rarely make the cut. So much for separate but equal, right. In addition, these low scoring schools are generally located in places where the property values are lower, therefore less property taxes are collected for school use.

Though New York City students are free to apply to any high school, the process rivals that of elite colleges, with costly essential prep classes for high-school entrance exams, and the better high schools cherry-picking the highest scorers, who are almost always

white or Asian students coming from the top middle schools. Mayor Bill de Blasio suggested Sunday, however, that changes are on the way. But for several graduating classes, this will prove too little, too late to help them in their educational pursuits.

Finally, it's been more than six decades since Brown v. the Board of Education, but school segregation is in the headlines on a daily basis. Schools have been moving back towards segregation in recent years. Nearly half of all African-American children attended majority white schools in 1988, which represented the pinnacle of desegregation in the U.S.

But in 2016, a Government Accountability Office report showed the number of African-American and Hispanic students in segregated schools to be rapidly climbing. According to that report, the number of high-poverty schools serving primarily African-American and Hispanic students more than doubled between 2001 and 2014. Throughout the country, schools are nearly as segregated as they were at the time of Brown v. the Board of Education decision.

This resegregation has been happening "behind the scenes," amid all the noise over standardized testing and implementing the Common Core. But recently the topic is dominating education policy discussions, partly due to the larger American focus on racism and inequality.

Over the past few decades, school districts have, one after other, seen their court-ordered desegregation orders expire. Since the beginning of the 21st century, hundreds of orders have lapsed, and virtually none have taken their place.

With New York City being one big exception, the situation is becoming severe in the South. Because districts there are often large, encompassing entire counties, it's hard not to have a diverse mix of students. But of late, some districts in the South have been breaking into smaller territories, due in part to predominantly white neighborhoods and towns "seceding" to form their own districts. Meanwhile, in other regions of the south, state governments are splintering large districts.

Now this is an interesting phenomenon. The school system I attended, my dad attended, my children, and now my grandson attends, is what is called in the Commonwealth of Kentucky as an "Independent" school district. Now, my parents, and myself when I was a property owner actually paid two tax bills when out taxes came due in December. By law, we had to pay school taxes to the County school system, and we also had to pay taxes to our "Independent" school district as well. For example, one year we received a $1200 tax bill, and over $1000 was taxes to the "Independent" school district.

Such was the case when Brown V Board of Education was decided. Thanks to years of systemic racism as well the practice of "redlining," where Blacks were not allowed to buy real estate in the same places their white counterparts could, condemning them to live in substandard housing and go to substandard schools. All the while, whites were making a beeline for the suburbs, along with higher property values as well as better educational opportunities for their children.

Today's student population is becoming increasingly diverse, yet American public schools are not reflecting that. Years after Brown v. Board of Education (1954) deemed school segregation unconstitutional in the United States, recent studies are showing that the vision of a desegregated school system has yet to be fully implemented. Even worse, a reality where segregation is a word for the history books is slipping further and further away.

Chapter Two

This report focuses primarily upon four important trends. First, the American South is resegregating, after two and a half decades in which civil rights law broke the tradition of apartheid in the region's schools and made it the section of the country with the highest levels of integration in its schools. Second, the data shows continuously increasing segregation for Latino students, who are rapidly becoming our largest minority group and have been more segregated than African Americans for several years. Third, the report shows large and increasing numbers of African American and Latino students enrolled in suburban schools, but serious segregation within these communities, particularly in the nation's large metropolitan areas. Since trends suggest that we will face a vast increase in suburban diversity, this raises challenges for thousands of communities. Fourth, we report a rapid ongoing change in the racial composition of American schools and the emergence of many schools with three or more racial groups. The report shows that all racial groups except whites experience considerable diversity in their schools but whites are remaining in overwhelmingly white schools even in regions with very large non-white enrollments.

According to the Civil Rights Project at the University of California, Los Angeles, the number of schools across the nation that are 90 to 100 percent nonwhite has more than tripled from 5.7 percent in 1988 to 18.4 percent in 2013. In California, 47.9 percent of African-American students attend 90–100 percent nonwhite schools. For Latino students in California, that statistic sits at 56.5 percent, the second worst rate in the nation behind New York's 56.8 percent.

Education and civil rights researchers point to a variety of reasons to explain this trend of increased segregation in the school system. Federal termination of desegregation plans in the early 1990s is one cause for the growing number of 90–100 percent nonwhite schools. In Board of Education of Oklahoma City Public Schools v. Dowell (1991), the Supreme Court found that the Board of Education had met federally mandated integration goals, and so the Court allowed for a permanent end to its government-sponsored desegregation plan. The Court held that "federal supervision of local school systems has always been intended as a temporary measure to remedy past discrimination." This decrease in regulation has at least partially lead to the resegregation students are experiencing today.

Though we usually think of segregation in racial and ethnic terms, it's important to also realize that the spreading segregation has a strong class component. When African-American and Latino students are segregated into schools where the majority of students are non-white, they are very likely to find themselves in schools where poverty is concentrated.

This is of course not the case with segregated white students, whose majority-white schools almost always enroll high proportions of students from the middle class. This is a crucial difference, because concentrated poverty is linked to lower educational achievement. School level poverty is related to many variables that effect a school's overall chance at successfully educating students, including parent education levels, availability of advanced courses, teachers with credentials in the subject they are teaching, instability of enrollment, dropouts, untreated health problems, lower college-going rates and many other important factors. The nation's large program of compensatory education, Title I, has had great difficulty achieving gains in schools where poverty is highly concentrated. When school districts return to neighborhood schools, white students tend to sit next to middle class students but black and Latino students are likely to be next to impoverished students.

Other contributing factors to the resegregation of American public schools are population change and the way neighborhoods are zoned for school attendance. The past 30 years have seen increasing populations of nonwhite students and decreasing white student populations within concentrated neighborhoods. These larger populations of nonwhite students, who also tend to be a part of lower socioeconomic groups, are likely to attend schools in low-income neighborhoods with low numbers of white students, leading to a phenomenon the Civil Rights Project researchers call "double segregation."

Students who attend segregated schools face a variety of barriers to success when compared to peers attending desegregated schools, including:

Less experienced and less qualified teachers

More teacher turnover

Worse school facilities and inadequate resources

Higher rates of student mobility

Fewer options for advanced curriculum

This leads to lower rates of academic achievement, poorer graduation rates and higher dropout rates.

Meanwhile, students who attend desegregated schools see:

Improved academic achievement, education attainment and occupational success

Lower levels of prejudice and stereotypical thoughts

Increased friendships across groups

Higher levels of civic engagement

Greater tendency to live and work in diverse environments as adults

Higher paying and more prestigious jobs

Better health

Decreased levels of adult poverty and incarceration

One economist at the University of California, Berkeley, has even found that attending a desegregated school can have multigenerational benefits. His research has also shown that while white students' test scores are not affected by attending a desegregated school, they benefit by cultivating measurably less racial prejudice and tend to live their adult lives in more integrated neighborhoods.

One aspect, which was not available in Pre-Brown educational systems, was the addition of many "centric" studies programs which have been added to both secondary and post-secondary educational institutions, this has given many students the opportunity to find out more about their own culture and exposure to such names as Marcus Garvey, W.E.B. Dubois, and countless others. This opportunity probably would or could not be afforded them if they were in an integrated classroom, as 1.) The teacher would most like be unqualified to teach it, 2.) Most students would view it as an extension of American History, and by leery to study it, and 3.) some parents would object to the subject matter, given the current state of xenophobia in the United States.

While this resegregation trend is unsettling, there are fortunately a growing number of California school districts with successful programs in place to support

African-American students, Latino students and other students of color. For instance, Sacramento City Unified School District's Blacks Making a Difference program provides mentoring and support to African-American students attending schools with large African-American student populations. In some northern and southern California high schools, the Puente Project program helps Latino students boost academic achievement and become college and career ready. These are just a few examples of how to advocate for these children.

Therefore, while debates over the exact academic impact of desegregation continue, there is no question that black and Latino students in racially integrated schools are generally in schools with higher levels of average academic achievement than are their counterparts in segregated schools. Desegregation does not assure that students will receive the better opportunities in those schools—that depends on how the interracial school is run, but it does usually put minority students in schools which have better opportunities and better prepared peer groups. In a period in which mandatory state tests for graduation are being imposed, college admissions standards are rising, remedial courses in college are being cut back, and affirmative action has already been abolished in our two largest states, the harmful consequences for students attending less competitive schools are steadily increasing.

We are clearly in a period when many policymakers, courts, and opinion makers assume that desegregation is no longer necessary, or that it will be accomplished somehow without need of any deliberate plan. Polls show that most white Americans believe that equal educational opportunity is being provided. National political leaders have largely ignored the growth of segregation in the 1990s. Thus, knowledge of trends in segregation and its closely related inequalities are even more crucial now. For example, increased testing requirements for high school graduation, for passing from one grade to the next, and college entrance can only be fair if we offer equal preparation to children, regardless of skin color and language. Increasing segregation, however, pushes us in the opposite direction because it creates more unequal

schools, particularly for low income minority children, who are the groups which most frequently receive low test scores. Educational policy decisions that do not take these realities into account will end up punishing students in inferior segregated schools, or even sending more children to such schools while simultaneously raising sanctions for those who do not achieve at a sufficiently high level.

In addition to its focus upon the trends of Southern resegregation, Latino student segregation and suburban segregation, this report documents basic national trends in enrollment and segregation for African-American students, Latinos, White and Asian students by region, by state, by community type allowing comparison across the country. In the final section, we offer recommendations on how to reverse the trend of rising segregation, concluding that there has been very little national leadership on this issue for the past quarter century, recalling the positive steps taken in the 1960s and 1970s, and suggesting a number of steps that would support successful desegregated schools.

So, is school segregation getting worse?

Plenty of people say yes, including scholars, journalists, and civil-rights advocates. For the first time in years, there's something approximating a consensus: Racially divided schools are a major and intensifying problem for American education, maybe even a crisis.

There's seemingly compelling numerical evidence, too. According to an analysis of data from the National Center on Education Statistics, the number of segregated schools (defined in this analysis as those schools where less than 40 percent of students are white), has approximately doubled between 1996 and 2016. In that same span, the percentage of children of color attending such a school rose from 59 to 66 percent. For black students, the percentage in segregated schools rose even faster, from 59 to 71 percent.

But not everyone is on board. In the eyes of some writers, the warning signs of segregation are all a false alarm—little more than a statistical mirage. The National Review writer Robert VerBruggen recently made this case, attacking what he called the "resegregation myth." VerBruggen and other skeptics contend that methods meant to identify school segregation are instead detecting something much more benign: The growing diversity of the American population.

This is possible because many measures of school segregation are narrow, focusing only on a single symptom. For instance, one common research technique is to count the number of schools above a certain demographic cutoff (for instance, more than 90 percent nonwhite). Another is to focus on "exposure," or how common it is for white and nonwhite students to encounter each other in the education system.

Doubters like VerBruggen argue that people using these metrics have been fooled by demographic change. The past several decades has seen a precipitous increase in the racial diversity of U.S. schoolchildren. For example, since 1996, the share of Hispanic and Asian students in public schools has grown from 17 to 31 percent. As a result, across the board, schools have tended to become less white.

This pretty much goes along with a statement I have made in my previous works, where I stated that by the year 2040, whites would be in permanently a minority in this country. As of today, August 23, 2020,

I was watching a program on CNN as a lead up to the Republican National Convention, one of the panelist stated that currently the 15 year old white person currently living in the U.S. is part of the majority/minority and will reach voting age by the 2024 Presidential election and if the Republican party wanted to remain viable, it would have to adapt a new message to these voters.

When diversity increases, some measures of segregation are likely to get worse, more or less by default. For instance, if an integrated school is growing, but most of the new students are Hispanic, at some point, it'll tip over and become segregated. If white students become a smaller share of the American population overall, all else equal, "exposure" to white students will probably decline.

VerBruggen claims that this shift, and little else, is responsible for the perceived crisis. "The rise in 'segregation' disappears when one measures segregation properly," he asserts. He and others say that, with slim evidence of increasing segregation, policies designed to proactively integrate schools are an obsolete form of social engineering.

It's a simple case. Too simple: There is plenty of evidence that resegregation is urgently real.

School segregation seems like it would be easy to gauge: Just add up the number of segregated schools, and see whether that number is going up or down over time. But the reality, unfortunately, is a lot more complicated.

The core problem is that the nation's schools are evolving in many ways at once. Student populations undergo slow shifts; new schools are constantly opening and closing; attendance boundaries are drawn and redrawn. As a result, the effects of large-scale demographic change and those of local school policy get tangled up with one another. It can be hard for researchers to separate one factor from the other.

Making things even tougher, increased national diversity tends to generate mixed signals about whether segregation is happening. As skeptics like Verbruggen point out, some measures of segregation, especially those that focus on the prevalence of white students, tend to look worse when student diversity increases. But other measures tend to look better. For example, one statistic known as a "dissimilarity index" calculates how many people would have to swap places to achieve demographic balance. When diversity increases evenly, dissimilarity indexes will improve—because the share of minority students in the least-integrated schools will grow, making fewer swaps necessary.

Contrary to the assertions of VerBruggen and others, there is broad statistical evidence of new racial stratification in schools. A recent (and helpfully illustrated) piece in Vox runs through some of that evidence, focusing on the changing role of attendance boundaries. The short version: Entire school districts are becoming more racially distinct from each other, even while racial diversity within those districts may be increasing.

In addition, while sweeping statistical indices have their uses, they tend to overlook some lower-level trends, like school openings and closures. That's a major blind spot when talking about the causes of new segregation. According to my analysis of the most recently available federal data, closures are about three times as common among segregated schools, and new schools account for a substantial share of current segregation. In 2016, 38 percent of all segregated schools had opened within the last two decades, compared to 20 percent of predominantly white and integrated schools. In at least this sense, nearly four-tenths of educational segregation is the result of students being shuffled into newly opened schools.

And there are other numbers that suggest a worsening trend. Almost everybody agrees that economic segregation is growing in schools, and many of those dubious about racial segregation like to advance this idea as a competing, alternative theory for educational inequality. But while income segregation can be simpler to measure than race, race and income are closely interwoven. The poorest schoolchildren are very disproportionately nonwhite; the poorest schools are usually racially segregated. The existence of economic segregation does not contradict evidence of racial segregation—it helps confirm it. It shows that, underneath the confounding effects of growing diversity, American school children are still being divided on the basis of social caste.

While resegregation skeptics are relying on oversimplified statistical evidence, there are even larger holes in their argument. One major reason civil-rights advocates fear resegregation is because they've directly observed changes to school policy that seem likely to contribute to racial isolation. Changes like this won't necessarily show up in statistical measures of student demographics—at least, not right away—but they're still important.

For example, most researchers believe that court-ordered integration plans, maintained by many school districts throughout the 1970s and 80s, were effective at reducing segregation. But since the turn of the century, hundreds of court orders have been terminated, and virtually no new ones have been created.

In places where segregation is already firmly established, government action can have the effect of "locking in" those racial lines. Here, an analogy might help: Imagine a housing subdivision where almost everyone is white, surrounded by neighborhoods that are heavily nonwhite. Now, imagine that the subdivision builds a large wall, hires a security guard for the entrance, and refuses to sell houses to anyone new. You'd be hard-pressed to argue these changes weren't segregative, even if, for the time being, everyone continues to live in the same place.

In American schools, metaphorical walls are going up all over the place. For instance, school districts in the south are traditionally larger than elsewhere in the country, often including entire counties. As a practical matter, this makes southern districts easier to integrate: Their wide expanse means they contain many white and nonwhite students alike. But in recent years, southern districts have begun to fragment. Sometimes this is caused by white neighborhoods and cities that attempt to "secede" and form their own, all-white districts. In other places, fragmentation is driven by statewide political forces, such as in North Carolina, where a conservative legislature is currently weighing breaking up large districts. No matter the cause, the ongoing splintering of districts places integration further out of reach.

In Memphis, Tennessee, for example, new racial lines are being drawn around the area's schools. In 2013 the majority-black Memphis city school district merged with the schools of the surrounding county, which were majority-white. At first blush, this was a move that promised integration. That is, until the next year, when six cities seceded from the merged district. Five of the six new districts are even whiter than the original county district had been, a new geography of segregation, freshly imposed. So even with the best of intentions, schools and segregation don't always work out the way the original planners had envisioned

And there are other ways to raise barriers to integration. In many big-city school districts, policymakers have spurred the growth of new charter schools to compete with traditional public schools. But because charters usually operate independently of the district they're in, students transferring into them can't be as easily included in a district's integration plans. This is another form of fragmentation, with charters acting as islands, administratively detached from the district around them. Perhaps not coincidentally, charters are also usually highly segregated, with students often sorted into distinct racial groups. Legal barriers are still barriers; this, too, is resegregation.

Underneath all of this is a deeper question: How much does the cause of segregation matter?

Imagine if a landlord, confronted with a leaking roof, responded by saying that the real problem is just too much rain. It's true that, in some sense, rain causes leaks—but only because there was something wrong with the roof in the first place. And at the end of the day, the leaks are still a problem that needs to be fixed.

Likewise, it's true that diversity in schools is increasing. But it's only making segregation worse because of flaws that already existed in the education system. The fundamental defect in American schools—the hole in the roof, if you will—is that they have long exhibited patterns of racial concentration, mostly due to housing segregation and decades of discriminatory education policy. If schools were already integrated to begin with, you'd expect increasing diversity to raise all boats relatively evenly. Most schools would get less white, but few would find themselves truly segregated. Instead, in a long-segregated system, the effects of increased diversity are inevitably lopsided. Schools already suffering from a relatively high degree of segregation have found themselves completely isolated.

Because of this, demographic changes are not experienced evenly. Because black students were already overrepresented in segregated schools, they often bear the brunt of an increase in racial isolation, whatever the proximate cause of those increases. That's why the share of black students in segregated schools has increased by 11 percent nationwide in the last two decades, faster than the share of either white students or nonwhite students overall, both of which have risen by about 6 percent, according to my analysis.

And, ultimately, there's just not much reason to think that identifying the exact cause of resegregation will ameliorate its harms. The vast majority of research into school segregation does not focus on its causes, but rather on the costs of attending a racially isolated school. There are many. They include reduced academic achievement, increased exposure to the criminal justice system, and significantly worsened professional and educational outcomes. Children in integrated schools find it easier to live and work in diverse environments; children in segregated schools are more prone to hold racially prejudiced views later in life. Racial isolation also tends to deprive children of color of what are sometimes obliquely called "networks of opportunity," in plain language, the day-to-day connections most people rely on to get a job or get into college.

And of course, there's another reason to worry about school segregation, regardless of its cause: the problem of second-class citizenship. Ironically, this problem generates less discussion than wonky, technocratic concerns about test scores and income mobility. But it was pivotal in propelling the school-integration push of the 1960s and 70s, and for good reason. Civil-rights advocates are not wrong to worry that, beyond any set of individual outcomes, it is not healthy nor sustainable for a society to effectively consign most children of color to an alternative system of schools. Doing so helps construct or reinforce ideas about racial caste in the minds of Americans — and, worst of all, in the minds of the children themselves.

None of these ills will heal themselves so long as segregated schools exist, or grow in number. And right now, such schools are growing in number, for reasons ranging from the benign to the nefarious.

Dedicated advocates and smart policymakers can thwart school resegregation, and eventually reverse it. But it will not reverse itself.

Chapter Three

At the beginning of the twentieth century, the great
black sociologist, W.E.B. DuBois, said that "The
problem of the twentieth century is the problem of the
color line." In the middle of this century the Supreme
Court directly challenged the color line in American
schools and began decades of political and legal
struggle over access for minority students to
integrated schools. For several decades it appeared
that a permanent turning point had been reached for
African American students as the South became the
nation's most desegregated region even through the
Reagan administration's efforts to end court orders,
desegregation continued to increase. By the 1990s
things began to turn back.

We have become a far more racially and ethnically
mixed nation, but in our schools, the color lines of
increasing racial and ethnic separation are rising.
There have not been any significant political or legal
initiative to offset this trend for a quarter century.
Although the Clinton Administration has seen the
largest increases in segregation in the last half
century, it has proposed no policies to offset the trend
and has not included the issue among its priorities for
education policy. Secretary Richard Riley's recent
speech on the 45th anniversary of the Brown case
praised the great decision but said nothing about the
increasing turn toward segregation. Most important,

the Supreme Court, which opened the possibility of desegregated education in the 1950s has taken decisive steps to end desegregation plans in the 1990s and some lower courts are prohibiting even voluntary local plans.

It has been 45 years since Brown v. Board of Education outlawed intentional segregation in the south, but a series of Supreme Court decisions in the 1990s helped push the country away from Brown's celebrated ideals and closer to the old idea of "separate but equal." Separate but equal was a concept articulated in the 1896 Plessy v. Ferguson Supreme Court decision that justified laws segregating schools and other institutions. Separate but equal was overturned six decades later by Brown's declaration that separate schools were inherently unequal. When the Supreme Court prohibited discrimination by state law in the 1950s, it called for only gradual change with "all deliberate speed" supervised by conservative Southern federal courts. During the next thirty years, however, the law developed in a series of decisions to require immediate

and complete desegregation in states with a history of official discrimination, even when busing was required to overcome residential segregation. In 1973, the Supreme Court in a case from Denver, Keyes v. School District No. 1, Denver, Colorado, extended desegregation requirements to Northern and Western cities with a history of local policies that fostered but did not directly

require segregation. This case also recognized the right of Latino as well as African American students to desegregated education. But the expansion of desegregation rights ended 25 years ago, with the Supreme Court's decision in Milliken v. Bradley, which would have desegregated students from the largely

minority city schools with suburban students in metropolitan Detroit. This rule was made in spite of findings of intentional discrimination by both state and local officials, which intensified segregation in the metropolitan area. Since many big cities, like Detroit, had rapidly declining white minorities in their schools, this meant that the large metropolitan areas with many separate

suburban school districts would lead the nation in segregation, which they continue to do today. In the second Detroit case, Milliken v. Bradley II, the Supreme Court seemed to offer a new version of separate but equal when it authorized federal courts to order money for programs in segregated schools to make up for the history of discrimination.

In the 1990s, a Supreme Court reconstructed by the appointees of Presidents Reagan and Bush handed down three very important decisions limiting desegregation rights and triggering a flood of lawsuits designed to end desegregation in major U.S.

districts. In the 1991 Dowell case the Court held that desegregation orders were temporary and that school boards could return to segregated neighborhood schools. The next year, in the Freeman v. Pitts decision the Court authorized piecemeal dismantling of desegregation plans. Finally, in the Jenkins case in 1995, the Court rejected the effort of a lower court to maintain the desegregation and magnet school remedy in the Kansas City case until it produced actual benefits for African American students, thus drastically limiting the reach of the separate but equal promise of Milliken II. According to the Supreme Court, the courts could order payments only for several years, and could not require that the programs produce measurable gains for the students subjected to a history of discrimination.

After the termination of court orders, under these recent decisions, the school districts would be declared "unitary" and free of all taint of discrimination. Once that happened, school boards were free to make decisions that had the effect of creating unequal opportunities for minority students unless civil rights lawyers could prove that they had intended to discriminate, a standard that is virtually impossible to meet. In addition, once a district is unitary, individual white parents can sue to try to prevent any conscious effort to maintain desegregation in any school, claiming that it discriminates against whites. Though the Supreme Court has not yet spoken on this issue, lower courts have ordered the end to special provisions to maintain interracial magnet schools in a number of districts. Some districts, like Boston, that bitterly fought desegregation for years, have now been forbidden to take voluntary steps under this doctrine. Many major school districts are in the process of phasing out their desegregation plans, so the trends reported in this study will surely accelerate in the next few years. Among school districts recently ending or phasing out their desegregation plans are a number of other major districts are now in litigation over the issue, with some of them struggling to be permitted to continue their desegregation plans.

Plessy permitted generations of unequal education and prompted decades of legal struggle against it. The resegregation decisions of our present period may well have a similar impact on the next century since there is considerable evidence that the resegregated schools of the nineties are profoundly unequal. We will examine changes in the racial composition of American schools, national patterns of segregation, the relationship between segregation by race and schools experiencing concentrated poverty, the difference in segregation in different regions and types of school districts, and the segregation of multiracial schools. For both African American and Latino students, the study reports differences in segregation by region and state and the most segregated states. The report concludes with a discussion of policies that could help reverse the trends toward intensifying segregation.

American schools are changing rapidly. The changes are the result of several factors including: the surge of non-European immigration since the 1965 law ending discriminatory immigration laws, the low birth rate among native whites, and much larger families among Latinos, who are the youngest population group. The steady rise in the proportion of minority children in our communities and their schools is not caused by white flight from public schools.

In 1996, 11% of U.S. students were in private schools, compared to 12% a half century earlier, before Brown, and 15% in the mid-1960s, just before significant desegregation began. Since the beginning of the civil rights era the proportion of Hispanics in the nation's public-school population has more than tripled. Census statistics for the 1940 to 1960 period show that non-white students totaled only 11 - 12% of the total enrollment. By 1996, the nonwhite enrollment was 36% and the Census Bureau projected that the total school age population would reach 58% non-white by 2050. Since the Office for Civil Rights of the Education Department began collecting national school data in 1968, the enrollment of Hispanics has increased by 218% while African Americans have grown more than a fifth and the white enrollment is down by a sixth (table 1). In the 1996-97 school year, the African American enrollment was 16.9% of the total enrollment and the Latino enrollment accounted for 14%.

The public schools of the U.S. foreshadow the dramatic transformation of American society that will occur in the next generation. We are a society in which the school age population is much more diverse than the older population. The social reality in our schools is far removed from the reality in our politics, since voters are older and much more likely to be white. When the modern school desegregation battles took shape in the 1950s, the issue was often described as the problem of opening up a white school system to the one-tenth of students who were black. Latino students received very little attention nationally and Asian students were a virtually invisible minority in a society that had prohibited Asian immigration for many decades. Today, Asians are nearly 4% of all students, and on a path to become one-tenth of the school population in mid-century, if existing trends continue. For the first time we have a large racial group whose average achievement scores and family incomes exceed those of whites, requiring us to rethink some of the assumptions about who benefits from desegregating with whom.

We already have five states where the majority of all public-school students are from "minority" backgrounds and these include our two largest and most influential states, California and Texas, which have produced four of the last six candidates elected President. In California, the Latino student body already slightly exceeds the white total in a state where one in nine students is of Asian origin, and one in eleven is black. The state has many schools where the integration is primarily between Latinos and Asians. Asians are far more likely than whites to be eligible for admission to the University of California system. The fact that African Americans are the second largest minority in Texas and the third largest in California is another sign of the need for a more complex way of thinking about segregation that takes multiracial schools into account.

Our largest city school systems now serve only a tiny minority of white students, but are extremely important for minority students. If we examine the largest big city school districts in 1996-97, we can see that in most of the largest districts several have 85% or more non-white enrollments and serve virtually no middle-class white families. Very few have more than one-third whites. One of the very serious problems facing education policy makers is that these school systems which are crucial for many millions of minority students, and face the most severe segregation by race and poverty, are of very little personal importance to the white population. Much of our recent school politics turns on various theories of why these schools are inferior and have not responded well to the reforms of the last generation. The core issues of racial and economic segregation are rarely mentioned in those political debates.

In terms of its total enrollment, the country by 1996 had two regions, the West and the South, where close to half the students were non-white and three regions, the Northeast, the Midwest, and the Border states, where there were large majorities of white students. All regions showed a decline in the percentages of whites in the student population but the change was by far the fastest in the West.

Change was the slowest in the whitest region, the Midwest, which has two of the nation's most segregated areas, metropolitan Chicago and metropolitan Detroit. In all parts of the national study of the largest federal school aid program, the Title I compensatory education program, noted that children in concentrated poverty schools receiving special aid actually performed better than those in less concentrated schools with no program. The Administration responded to that finding by recommending more dollars for isolated schools and there was no discussion of possible strategies for lowering the intensity of the isolation, there would be less contact with whites even if there were full desegregation because there is a slowing declining percentage of school age whites. This explanation for increasing segregation is most relevant in the West where the decline in the percentage of white students far outstripped the other regions between 1987 and 1996. There was an 8.9% reduction of white enrollment in the West compared to a ~4.5% reduction in all other regions. This trend, a 1%

decrease in white enrollment each year, could result in the West becoming the first region to have a white minority in its public schools by the year 2001.

Historically, the South has always had the highest proportion of black students. The South (the eleven states of the old Confederacy) is the nation's most populous region, with 13.7 million students, of whom 27.4% are black. The six Border states and the District of Columbia, which also mandated racial segregation until 1954, have 19.7% black students. The regions with the lowest proportions of black students are the West with 6.5% and the Midwest with 13.7%.

Since the proportion of blacks to whites is highest in the South, and the integration effort has been more intense, in the South, the amount of contact whites have with blacks is considerably higher than elsewhere the U.S. Examining the list of states where whites have the highest contact with non-whites in their schools, one finds that they are all in the formerly de jure segregated states. The only state outside the South on this list is Delaware, which also had de jure segregation and was one of the only states ordered to desegregate across city-suburban boundary lines. Although there has been a great deal of criticism of excessive integration elsewhere, none of the northern states had white children in schools with an average of even one-sixth combined black and Latino children. During the civil rights era, southern whites often complained that northerners were unwilling to desegregate their own communities. That proved to be true.

The white proportion of student enrollment is dropping rapidly in some areas, suggesting that white students should be coming into contact with more minority students. Yet white segregation remains very high. Although the nation's two largest states, California and Texas, have a majority of non-white students, neither shows high levels of integration for white students.

The huge growth of Latino enrollment is concentrated in a few states. A substantial majority of all Latinos in the country attend school in the nation's two largest states, California and Texas, which have 3.7 million of the 6.4 million Latino pupils, 58% of the total.

Since 1954, after the Supreme Court outlawed segregation in southern schools, we are past the high point of desegregation and a decade into the resegregation of public schools. The most important trends in this report are the accelerating resegregation of the South and the continuation of a long and relentless march toward even more severe segregation for Latino students as they become our largest minority. The study also shows large enrollments of African American and Latino students in the suburbs and serious suburban segregation, particularly in the nation's large metropolitan areas. The segregation that is spreading in the nation is not just segregation by race. Segregated African American and Latino schools are many times more likely than white schools to face concentrated poverty, which is powerfully related to lower educational results. The South has always been the heartland of African Americans, home to a majority of blacks, it had the most integrated schools in the U.S. for more than a quarter century. The civil rights movement was mostly a struggle about the seventeen southern and border states with apartheid laws. The courts required a much higher standard of proof to obtain desegregation outside the South and never developed a workable remedy for the large metropolitan areas of the North. Some of the most desegregated southern states are now moving rapidly backward.

In 1954, the Supreme Court responded to the history of discrimination in the seventeen states that mandated segregation in an eloquent ruling. The Court's Brown v. Board of Education decision held that denial of access to equal public education violated the basic rights of students and that segregation must end. Nearly ninety years after the Civil War and sixty years after Plessy v. Ferguson, seventeen states and Washington, D.C. still had official and total racial segregation of their public schools. The Court held that such segregation was "inherently unequal" and caused irreversible harm. This was probably the most important Supreme Court decision of the twentieth century, bringing back to life the anti-discrimination amendments to the Constitution enacted during Reconstruction, and creating a new sense of possibilities in the country about ending the apartheid that had shaped the lives of most blacks. "Separate but equal" had been tried for a century and failed, producing a momentum of growing educational inequality. Brown demanded a new start. The Supreme Court put off its decision about how to enforce Brown until 1955 and then called for gradual change "with all deliberate speed." When Southern states refused to comply, it became necessary to sue each individual district. The district courts ordered very gradual implementation of limited "freedom of choice" plans which left the black schools segregated and permitted a few African American children to attend white schools. Ninety-eight percent of Southern black children were still in totally segregated schools in 1964. The great progress in desegregation came from the mid-1960s to the early 1970s, after the enactment of the 1964 Civil Rights Act and following a series of Supreme Court decisions tightening requirements, ending delay, and authorizing busing. Slow progress continued through much of the 1960s. By 1970, the enforcement of the 1964 civil rights act by the Johnson Administration and the courts had made the South the nation's most integrated region for both blacks and whites. The integration was deep and durable, in spite of major policy changes ending enforcement of desegregation by the executive branch.

After nearly a quarter century of increasing integration, the tide turned in the other way in the late 1980s. That process of resegregation has continued through the 1996-97 school year. The percent of black students in majority white schools in the South fell from a peak of 43.5% down to 34.7% in 1996, a clear and consistent eight year decline (table 8), with integration falling below the level achieved 24 years earlier, in 1972. In this report the South refers to the 11 states of the old Confederacy and the Border states are the six slave states Oklahoma, Missouri, Kentucky, West Virginia, Maryland, and Delaware that stayed with the Union but enforced

segregation laws until after the Brown decision. In these tabulations, the District of Columbia is included in the Border states.

The basic patterns of segregation in the history of the last half century in the South are a very gradual beginnings of desegregation for black students in the 1950s, a dramatic breakthrough from the middle 1960s through the busing decisions of the early 1970s, a continued increase in interracial contact through several administrations attacking urban desegregation plans, followed by an accelerating process of resegregation since the late 1980s. During the entire period of rapid increase in desegregation, the Supreme Court had limited its attention to the states with segregation laws, the 17 Southern and Border states. Commenting on earlier reports of reversals of desegregation, some observers have concluded that the Supreme Court's effort was futile and that things are worse off than they were before

1954. Although the current trend is moving toward higher levels of segregation, that conclusion is wholly unwarranted. When the Supreme Court acted, there was virtually total segregation across a vast region. In the 1996-97 school year, the South is still the nation's most integrated region. (For those who despair in looking at black educational problems today, it is also important to observe that since the early 1950s, the black high school graduation rate has tripled across the U.S.) In spite of the serious reverses reported here, there is no doubt that a great deal was achieved by desegregation and other education reforms, and that the largest gains often came for African American students in the South. Nothing here suggests a return to the absolute segregation that prevailed in the South in 1950, but Southern black students are likely to experience less and less contact with whites.

The national trends have parallels with the Southern trends. American schools continue the pattern of increasing racial segregation for black and Latino students. The percent of black students in majority white schools peaked in the early 1980s and declined to the levels of the 1960s by the 1996-97 school year. In terms of intense segregation, this number has turned up only in the more recent past and the increase has been modest. Latino segregation by both measures has grown steadily throughout the past 28 years, surpassing the black level in predominantly non-white schools by 1980 and slightly exceeding the proportion in intensely segregated schools (90-100%

minority) in the 1990s. Residential segregation has been substantially lower for Latinos than for blacks but the school segregation statistics show that the next generation of Latinos are experiencing significantly less contact with non-Latino whites; 45% of Latinos were in majority white schools in 1968 but only 25% in 1996. Latino student attended a school with 43.8% whites in 1970, but the number is down sharply to 29.9% in the new data. Blacks, on the other hand, are back to where they were in the early 1970s, after experiencing more interracial schools in the 1980s. We do not have national segregation statistics for African Americans from the 1950s because the data was not collected in the North. Given the fact that a substantial majority of African Americans lived in the South, however, where the schools were totally segregated at that point, African Americans are doubtless still in less segregated schools than they were almost a half century ago.

For Latinos, however, the conclusion that segregation is worse than at the time of Brown is probably more accurate, though we do not have national statistics until more than a decade after Brown. The right of Latinos to desegregation was not even recognized by the Supreme Court until 19 years after Brown and it was never vigorously enforced. (There had been earlier legal rulings in the 1940s against de jure segregation of Latinos in parts of the Southwest, but no positive duty to desegregate emerged until the Supreme Court's 1973 decision). The steady growth of segregation, since federal data was first collected, has only been interrupted in Colorado and in Texas following busing orders. Elsewhere in the nation, the growth has been very large. In 1970 the average Latino student was in a school with a little over half non-white students (56%), but in 1996 the average Latino was in a 70% non-white school.

Chapter Four

Most reports about segregation since 1954 have primarily studied the isolation of black students from white students. During the past two decades there have been a series of reports by Gary Orfield which have also consistently reported Latino segregation statistics, though those received far less attention. Isolation from whites is obviously a very important issues in a predominantly white society, where the major institutions are controlled by whites, but statistics do not provide a full picture of an increasingly multiracial nation. One obvious question is: if non-white children are not in schools with whites, are they in school with children of their own racial group or a mix of non-whites? And as for whites, though they are, on average, in schools, with 81% white classmates, how much exposure do they have to each of the other groups?

It turns out that based on the national average, the average white student is in a school with 8.6% black students, 6.6% Latinos, 2.8% Asians, and 1% American Indians. Whites are the only racial group that attends schools where the overwhelming majority of students are from their own race. Blacks and Latinos attend schools where a little more than half the children are from their own group, on average, while American Indians attend schools that are one-third Indian [excluding Bureau of Indian

Affairs (BIA) schools]. Asians tend to be in schools that are only about a fifth Asian. Black schools have about a tenth Latino students, on average, while Latino schools have about a ninth African American students. Asians and American Indian public-school students are in schools with a much larger number of whites (almost half) than other non-white groups. Both Asians and American Indians attend schools with far more Latinos than blacks, reflecting the racial composition of the West.

When I graduated back in ancient times from High School (that is according to my grandson, who could not believe I started working on computers way back in 1981, when I was a junior in High School,) our school system was lily-white, there was only one young lady who was a refugee from Laos, so my High School was something like 99.99% white. I wasn't exposed to other cultures or other races until I was well into my college experience. After that, I attempted to make friends or at least acquaintances with people who were different than I. As time progressed, my high school became more diverse and I encouraged my children to make friends with people from other races and cultures. I tried and I think I was fairly successful in raising two tolerant young adults. Now my grandson has a friend that is Black, a couple who are Hispanic, and one I believe is from India. His mother did not have to teach him tolerance of other cultures, as it was as normal to him as his own. But I have had to teach him the positives of being Appalachian American (Yes, us Hillbillies are a recognized minority group.) So, yes, I did go to a segregated school system, but it was segregated because the population of the school system was white, and working class. When I was younger, I could not figure out why Blacks (I had no knowledge of the existence of Hispanics or any other races,) did not settle in my school district, it wasn't until I was older when I found out the truth. If a Black family happened to try to move in, they were discouraged by the realtors because the citizens of the two towns did not want their property values to go down. Basically, Blacks were "redlined" out of my school system, that is until a cardiologist was brought in by one of the major employers, and that cardiologist just so happened to be Black. Suddenly, doors were opened that had been previously closed. That cardiologist is my parent's Primary Care Physician, and he takes care of my parents very well.

We have many schools emerging with types of interracial and multiracial populations that have received virtually no attention from policy makers or researchers, but will doubtless have a significant impact on relationships between these groups. Many teachers and administrators are already working in kinds of schools neglected in both policy and in research. Many more will be in the future. Students in such schools go to school in highly complex and dynamic environments, and whose complex interactions are poorly understood. In an increasingly

multiracial America, we will need to think about the
degree to which different groups of student are
concentrated in schools with other students who have
higher or lower achievement levels. Blacks, Latinos,
and American Indians are the groups of students
experiencing the greatest educational problems in the
schools. Blacks and Latinos, on average, are in schools
where 65% of the students are black, Latino, or
Indian. Asians, on the other hand, tend to be in
schools where 31% of the students are black, Latino,
or Indian, and whites attend schools where just 16%
are from these groups. Segregation also has
implications for the level of exposure an immigrant
student has to English-speaking students and to
students speaking his/her own language. Asian
students are, of course, much less likely to be isolated
by language, being in schools where an average of
four-fifths of the students are not Asian, thus they
interact with many native English speakers. Latino
immigrants, however, are much more likely to be in
heavily Latino schools with a much higher proportion
of native language speakers and a lower share of
fluent English speakers. Thus, when compared with
Latino and black students, Asians, on average,
experience a high degree of integration with groups
of students who tend to have higher average
achievement levels and less linguistic isolation. There
are stark differences, however, within the Asian
population. Asians who lived in this country prior to
the end of the Vietnam war tended to be wealthier
and more educated than the large refugee groups

who arrived after the war. So, while the average Asian faces a much more integrated picture than the average black or Latino student, there are large numbers of Asian students who live in very segregated high poverty situations. Asian segregation in the nation is growing significantly.

Concentrated poverty is strongly linked to many forms of educational inequality. Black and Latino students, on average, attend schools with more than twice as many poor classmates as white students and Asians and American Indian students are about halfway in-between. Latinos have the highest average percentage of impoverished classmates (46%), compared to 19% for whites.

The 1996 data also show that 47% of U.S schools still had between 0-10% black and Latino students and that only one in 14 (7.7%) of those schools had half or more of their children living in poverty. On the other extreme, 8% of schools were intensely segregated with between 90-100% black and Latino Students. Of those schools, 87% of the children were impoverished.

In other words, the students in the segregated minority schools were 11 times more likely to be in schools with concentrated poverty and 92% of white schools did not face this problem. This relationship is absolutely central to explaining the different educational experiences and outcomes of the schools. A great many of the educational characteristics of schools attributed to race are actually related to poverty but the impacts are easily confused since in most metropolitan areas there are few if any concentrated poverty white schools while the vast majority of segregated black or Latino schools experience such poverty and all the educational differences that are associated with it. These issues are often confused, for example, in the statement by minority critics of desegregation who claim, correctly, that there is nothing magic about sitting next to a white child, but sometimes end up advocating policies that put their children in inferior concentrated poverty schools.

Often different regions of the country have had differing trends in desegregation. The different legal situations in the South and North and the smaller and more fragmented districts in parts of the country tend to produce differing outcomes. From the mid-1960s through the mid1980s, the gains in desegregation were by far the largest in the 17 Southern and Border states with a history of segregation laws, because the enforcement effort was focused there. In examining the trends between 1991 and 1996, however, a historic shift had occurred and these were the regions with the largest increases in segregation.

The recent increase in segregation for black students was the sharpest in the regions, which have historically been the most integrated parts of the U.S. since 1970, and have had the largest percentage of black students in their enrollment. Statistics for African American segregation show that it declined substantially in a number of states with large black enrollments during the busing era of the 1970s, but that it began to increase significantly since 1980. The largest declines in segregation came in Delaware and Kentucky which both implemented city suburban desegregation plans in the big metropolitan area where most of their minority students lived (Wilmington and Louisville). These two states did not have large percentages of minority populations, were rich states, and also happen to be the two most suburban states in the country. Missouri, where the other significant city-suburban desegregation plan was implemented in metropolitan St. Louis, also experienced a very substantial drop in the level of black segregation. Ohio, which had new orders in its major cities also had a major decline, as did Wisconsin after the implementation of the Milwaukee desegregation plan. The other state with a significant decline was Oklahoma where Oklahoma City desegregated. In Connecticut and New Jersey, blacks and Latinos tended to be left behind in highly segregated, very poor and seriously declining central cities surrounded by wealthy suburban rings. In both of these states, metropolitan areas are fragmented into large numbers of small districts. After the Supreme Court's decision in 1974 blocking city-suburban desegregation, little additional progress took place in many states.

Between 1980 and 1996, Indiana, which implemented city-suburban desegregation in 1980 showed the only large drop in segregation. The Indianapolis plan began to be phased out in 1998 when the Justice Department decided to settle the case under a plan that provided no long-term school desegregation. Missouri was the only other state to continue to increase integrated education significantly. The St. Louis case was settled in 1998 under an unusual plan that will continue substantial desegregation for another decade but then phase it out. Virtually all the other states with substantial black enrollments show rising segregation since 1980. The largest increases came in Rhode Island (20%), Wisconsin (13%), Florida (12%), Oklahoma (12%), Maryland (9%), Delaware (9%), and Massachusetts (9%).

The most segregated states in the U.S. for black students have included Michigan, Illinois and New York for many years. New Jersey has traditionally been in the top four most segregated states, but that ranking slipped a little, though the state still ranks 5th on two of the three measures. Examining segregation in 1996, it is apparent that California and Maryland have moved into the top levels of black segregation in the country even though California has less than a tenth black students. At the peak of Southern desegregation, there were no southern states near the top of the list. Now we see four of the states of the old South; Mississippi, Alabama, Louisiana, and Texas — as among the most segregated states.

Some states with very low black enrollment still are highly segregated. There are 18 states with less than

6% black enrollment. Of these states, Minnesota has the highest proportion of its black students in majority non-white schools, closely followed by three states in the Southwest, Arizona, Colorado and New Mexico, all of which have large Latino enrollments and much larger total minority enrollments. In addition to Minnesota there is a surprising level of

segregation in the Pacific Northwest. Oregon has only 2.5% black students and Washington has only 4.8% but in each state nearly a third of those students are in majority non-white schools. Minnesota also reported that by 1996, 6.8% of its black students were in intensely segregated schools with more than nine-tenths minority students. The biggest cities in both Washington and Minnesota have recently voted to dissolve their desegregation plans and return to segregated neighborhood schools, so these levels of isolation will certainly rise in the future. One other state deserving attention is Utah. With the lowest percent of black students in the nation, 7/10 of 1%, Utah has managed to put an eighth of these students in predominantly minority schools.

Some states show dramatic declines in integration in the last five-year period, particularly

Maryland and Rhode Island. Others, where major desegregation plans have been ended or are

being phased out since 1996 will probably show similar increases in the 1998 or 2000 data. In Maryland there has been a very large black migration to the suburbs and segregation has risen substantially in the two largest Washington suburban counties, Prince George's and Montgomery. Prince George's has recently terminated its desegregation plan so there should be further intensification there. Montgomery had a very modest voluntary plan that has not forestalled increased segregation of both blacks and Latinos and it has been sued because of a policy attempting to integrate magnet programs. Baltimore schools have been overwhelmingly black for many years. Latino segregation has been increasing ever since data was first collected in the 1960s but the issue has never received much attention since the great increase came after the civil rights era. Nearly twenty years after Brown the Supreme Court recognized in the 1973 Denver decision that Latinos had faced a history of segregation and were entitled to a desegregated education.

There never was a significant effort to enforce this right, however, and substantial desegregation for Latinos occurred in only a few places. Latino students are significantly more segregated than African Americans and segregation has been rapidly growing in the states where they have the largest enrollments.

Segregation leaves Latino students in schools with high levels of concentrated poverty, low average levels of competition and low levels of college enrollment. Latino students have by far the highest dropout rates of any major group in American schools and are experiencing declining access to college in an era in which post-secondary education is absolutely crucial for good jobs. Part of the reason is that they attend schools with far higher concentrations of poverty than other racial and ethnic groups and these schools tend to have very low performance levels, fewer teachers teaching in their subject areas, and many other forms of inequality. The Northeast continues to be the most segregated region for Latinos, largely reflecting the situation in the consolidated New York metropolitan area.

The South and the West are just behind the Northeast, which was far more segregated than other regions in the past. The West, where Latinos are the dominant minority group has a substantial increase in segregation and now has 77% of Latino children in predominantly minority schools. A very substantial share of Latinos are now attending intensely segregated (90-100% non-white) schools — 46% in the Northeast, 38% in the South, and 33% in the West, where this level of segregation was uncommon two decades ago.

The scope of the changes in Latino segregation has not been widely recognized because Latinos are concentrated in the Southwest, where they play a very large and historic role in the society. In the Washington, D.C. area and many of the major regions of the East, the Latino presence is much lower. There are also large numbers in Florida, New York, New Jersey and Illinois, but these populations tend to be highly concentrated in the largest metropolitan areas and have much less visibility across the state.

Texas has a history of much more rigid segregation of Latinos than does California and was the location for most of the civil rights cases against segregated Latino schools. In 1970, Latino children attended California schools with an average of 54% white enrollment. But by 1996, they were in schools where the average white enrollment had plummeted to 23.5% and 76.5% of the students were "minorities." Texas and Colorado Latinos actually had an increase in integration from 1970 to 1980, probably from busing orders, but Texas was one of the first states to end its urban desegregation plans and Latinos were more segregated by 1996 than they had been 26 years earlier. Colorado Latinos were far more integrated than those in the other Southwestern states through 1996, but since then the federal court has ended desegregation in Denver and state law forbids busing for desegregation without a federal court order. New York, on the other extreme, had consistently high segregation throughout the entire period.

Since federal data was first collected, New York has been the most segregated state for Latino students on all three measures used in this study. The typical Latino student attends a school where less than a fifth of the students are white and only one-eighth are in majority white schools in a state with a large majority of white students. New York has traditionally had much higher levels of residential segregation for

Latinos than other states. California, which was much less segregated a quarter century ago, is rapidly approaching the New York level of hyper segregation, as is Texas. Predominantly Puerto Rican and Dominican areas tend to show very high segregation levels and New Jersey and Connecticut's cities fall into this pattern. The Illinois pattern largely reflects the extreme segregation of the Chicago public schools and the rapid increase of the Latino community there. This brings us back to the only state with a high level of Latino enrollment that does not show severe segregation in 1996! Colorado. The Denver case was the one in which the right of Latinos to desegregated education was recognized by the Supreme Court. In 1997, however, the Federal District Court approved permitting Denver to return to segregated neighborhood schools.

Those examining the causes of the increase in Latino segregation may well ask whether or not it is simply a reflection of the rising share of Latinos in the school age population and the declining share of whites, since there never were many desegregation plans aimed at ending Latino segregation. The answer to this question is yes, a large share of the increase is demographic and full desegregation in majority white schools is no longer a possibility in some states. A new analysis for the U.S. National Center for Education Statistics shows that much of the decline in desegregation could be accounted for by the growth of the Latino enrollment between 1987 and 1996.

It is important to recall, however, that whites remain highly segregated in the regions of rapid Latino enrollment growth, which would not be expected if this were merely due to demographic changes acting uniformly across districts. Since the early days of urban desegregation many critics have claimed that desegregation was impossible, that white flight from desegregation plans made them highly unstable, and that the whole thing was an exercise in futility. The fact that most national opinion leaders are located in two great metropolitan areas means that the experiences of Washington D.C. and New York City are often treated as if they are typical of the country, when nothing could be further from the truth. In fact, the 1996 data shows that 55% of blacks and 67% of Latino students lived in large metropolitan areas and another fourth of the population of each group lived in small metropolitan areas. Those who lived in rural areas, in towns, and in small communities were by far the most integrated. Blacks and Latinos in the central cities of large metropolitan areas, on the other hand were by far the most segregated. In a society which is now dominated by the suburbs, it is extremely interesting that 30% of Latinos and 20% of blacks are now enrolled in the suburban schools of large metropolitan areas, and another 6% attend school in the suburbs of smaller metropolitan areas. The population growth of minority students is going to be overwhelmingly suburban if the existing trends continue. One of the most important questions for the next generation will be whether or not the suburbs will repeat the experience of the central cities or learn how to operate stable integrated schools. Table 22 shows that suburban blacks and Latinos in large metropolitan areas are already attending schools that have an average non-white enrollment of 60% for blacks and 64% for Latinos, though this is twice the level of contact with whites that occurs in central city schools. Suburban whites in the large metro areas, on the other hand, attend schools with an average of 6.8% blacks and 7.4% Latinos, less than half the level of central city whites. The suburbs of small metropolitan areas are considerably more integrated for blacks, but not for Latinos.

The areas most affected by changes in desegregation law have been the Southern and Border states, where civil rights enforcement beginning in the mid-1960s created wide-scale integration of black students. The impact of civil rights enforcement was greatest there for three reasons. First, the previous segregation was by far the most extreme, a true apartheid system under state segregation laws that had been fiercely defended by state and local officials and

which had changed only slowly until Congress acted in 1964. Second, lower courts developed desegregation policies that were easy to enforce in the formerly de jure states that had explicit segregation laws. But in other states, where segregation had been achieved not through such explicit laws, it required more effort to document and pinpoint discrimination. Third, black students in the South were far less likely than their northern counterparts to be concentrated in big cities and the South's school district organization combines cities and suburbs in a metropolitan area. This is vastly different than other regions, which fragment their metropolitan communities into small segregated pieces. As late as 1964, 98 percent of Southern black students and nearly all Southern white students had attended segregated schools. The enactment of the 1964 Civil Rights Act, the active enforcement of that law by the Johnson Administration, and major Supreme Court decisions tightening desegregation requirements made the South the most integrated region in the country by 1970. The Supreme Court decisions that required desegregation plans to end segregated schools by student reassignment and busing produced huge changes.

Currently the school districts terminating desegregation or in court over the issue are some of the largest metropolitan districts in the South and most of the big cities with outstanding court orders outside the South. The only offsetting force is the rapid suburbanization of the black and Latino middle class. Whether or not this will produce lasting integration or merely a vast spread of suburban segregation is one of the great questions of this period. Unfortunately, there is no policy and no assistance for these racially-changing communities and an almost total absence of discussion among school districts about changes that will require

regional responses if we want to avoid the sorry
experiences of the intense segregation in the central
cities. No such discussions are taking place. The U.S.
is more multiracial than ever before and is in the
midst of a demographic transformation. It makes
sense, then, that we should be working to understand
and foster successful multiracial schools. The states
that have already become predominantly minority
have not launched any initiatives to accommodate the
changes. In California, for example, instead of a
focused discussion about multiracial community-
building, the loss of the white

majority spawned a sweeping attack on Latinos' civil
rights and a termination of virtually all the state's
desegregation plans. Texas has also been aggressive
in ending urban desegregation plans. Both Texas and
California have eliminated affirmative action at the
college level. Texas has imposed test requirements for
high school graduation and had the nation's second
highest high school dropout rate in 1996. Both states
have enacted increasingly demanding testing systems
while concentrating more and more of their urban
students in highly segregated schools. The new white
minority in the schools, which will eventually become
a white minority in politics, can only hope that the
non-white populations show greater regard for access
by minority whites than white leaders did for them.
The Clinton Administration has presided over a
period of substantial and continuous increase in
segregation without any initiatives to offset these

trends. No significant litigation has been filed; the Justice Department agreed to a very weak settlement of its only metropolitan

desegregation case, there has been no effort to restore the desegregation aid program that the Reagan administration cancelled and no new major research on race relations, segregation, or desegregation in American schools. The President's race initiative came up with no significant recommendations that would address increasing segregation. Although the Congressionally mandated study of Title I showed that Title I programs work very poorly in concentrated poverty schools, there has never been any proposal to reduce concentrations of poverty. The current Administration affirms its support for integrated schools but has no set of policies that would foster or support them, no research program to learn how to help them work better, no aggressive legal strategy to fight against segregation and no critical discussion of the impact of the current pro-segregation court decisions on the country and no plan to help stabilize

integration in hundreds of racially changing suburban school districts. During the past year, the Justice Department agreed to abandonment of city-suburban desegregation opportunities in Indianapolis—the only midwestern metropolitan area with substantial desegregation—without so much as a trial. The administration's policies and seeming lack of concern about segregation implies an acceptance of a "separate but equal" strategy in public schools. Though the Clinton Administration is interested in interracial colleges through support of affirmative action, if more and more minority students are educated in less competitive schools, and the administration's favored policies against "social promotion" and in favor of high stakes tests are enacted, these minority students will not be ready to succeed in college. This is the first Democratic

administration in 40 years that has had no program for school integration. Previous administrations took positive actions. For example: Kennedy: Proposed major new civil rights laws greatly expanding Federal enforcement power against segregated schools.

Johnson: Enacted laws and enforced them more vigorously than any previous or subsequent administration. Brought the South from almost total segregation to give it the nation's most desegregated schools.

Nixon: Though opposed to busing, supported federal desegregation aid program to support successful operation of interracial schools enacted in 1972. Research showed clear benefits until the program was ended by Reagan Administration.

Carter: Expanded and greatly improved desegregation aid program and research. Actively resisted rollback of urban desegregation and initiated combined housing and school desegregation strategies. After 12 years of intense and focused opposition to desegregation orders under Presidents

Reagan and Bush and successful confirmation of hundreds of conservative federal judges, the law now is much closer to Reagan's vision than to that of the Warren and Burger Courts. Mandatory desegregation orders are being dissolved on a large scale and voluntary ones are being challenged in many courts. There has been no significant countervailing intellectual, political or legal force from the Clinton Administration that might reverse trends.

In order to buck these trends, there must be an alternative to the current policies. Some priorities for avoiding massive resegregation and improving interracial schools would include:

1) active discussion and leadership on this issue by the President and Education and Justice Department leaders, who would explain trends and consequences and discuss constitutional issues. Initiatives of this sort by the Reagan Administration, together with a systematic restaffing of the courts, have produced the current legal changes that exacerbate segregation.

2) leadership by the Justice Department and the Office for Civil Rights in defining standards for "unitary status" which specify how the various legal requirements of desegregation should be factually examined. Also important is the use of educational expertise to help the courts, which are often making

quick and superficial judgments of complex issues, related to schools.

3) aggressive defense of remaining court orders.

4) requirements that charter schools receiving federal funds are desegregated in conformity with local and state desegregation plans and policies.

5) incentives in Title I plans that facilitate and encourage the transfer of low-income students from concentrated-poverty low-achieving schools to schools that are more diverse. This is logical, since Title I research shows little success of Title I programs in concentrated poverty schools, which are usually segregated minority schools.

6) a policy of strong support for diverse suburban communities by the Education, HUD, and Justice Departments. This would include research on successful local practices that create integrated communities and vigorous enforcement against housing market and lending practices that spread segregation.

7) proposing a program of aid for human relations, staff training, and educational reform in the nation's thousands of multiracial schools. Such a program existed until the Reagan Administration eliminated it.

8) fill the vacant federal judgeships.

We are floating back toward an educational pattern that has never in the nation's history produced equal

and successful schools. There is no good evidence that
it will work now. The 1990s have actually seen the
once shrinking racial achievement gaps begin to
widen again on some tests. It is clear, that the
Administration's favored educational policies in place
are not likely to produce equal segregated schools.
Reversing the trends of intensifying segregation and
inequality will be difficult, but the costs of passively
accepting them are likely to be immense.

Chapter Five

Indeed, a recent study of metropolitan segregation found that D.C. is actually towards the middle of the pack in terms of segregation, considerably better than the most segregated American city, Milwaukee. It's also no accident, segregation everywhere reflects residues of deliberate government policy, mainly in the form of enormous subsidies of white enclaves, and measures to corral black residents in impoverished ghettos. The least segregated cities are generally newer ones, built after redlining and other forms of discriminatory policy were repealed.

But segregation is still immensely harmful, worsening poverty, directly causing sickness (particularly asthma and lead poisoning), poor student outcomes, and more. It's long since time for a return to bold integration policy, for housing and for schools.

Let me start with schools. After the civil rights movement, liberals generally agreed that something needed to be done to remedy the legacy of Jim Crow in addition to restoring voting rights for African-Americans in the South. Black schools, in particular, were systematically overcrowded and underfunded. One common solution for hundreds of school districts trying to comply with federal court orders to desegregate was to shuffle some students around between districts to create a reasonable racial balance.

In a truly classic American tradition, whites across the country, South and North alike; Boston's Louise Day Hicks was probably the most prominent anti-integration activist, reacted with purple-necked fury. They coined a slogan which supposedly described their resentment: "forced busing." The implication was that this new use of busing was coercing parents and children into attending schools other than their local neighborhood schools. It fit nicely into developing neoliberal notions of government policy being illegitimate intrusions into "natural" free market outcomes.

Unfortunately, as Matt Delmont shows in his brilliant book Why Busing Failed, all this anti-busing rhetoric was duplicitous garbage. As Jake Blumgart summarizes:

The number of children transported to school by bus had been increasing steadily for decades before Brown v. Board of Education, often as a means to enforce segregation. (The plaintiff in Brown was bused 20 miles to a majority-black school despite the majority-white school four blocks from her home.) In Boston, 85 percent of high school students were bused before school integration efforts began. Only when the form of transportation became associated with desegregation did some parents object to it and heap praise on "neighborhood schools."

These court orders worked quite well at cutting segregation. But — assisted by the widespread acceptance of the ridiculous "forced busing" frame — the racist backlash resulted in several anti-integration bills passing Congress, and most school districts eventually wormed their way out from under court orders.

The result was quick and pervasive resegregation. A sample of 159 schools across the South began to see increased segregation levels only a few years after they were released from federal court oversight. Within about a decade, segregation levels were just as bad or worse than they had been before. An investigation into the five worst elementary schools in Florida found the exact same procedure to blame. Measured by the percentage of black students in schools that are 90 percent minority or more, segregation has increased in all regions of the country since the mid-'80s (when court orders were most common). Indeed, the Northeast's segregation has increased compared to 1968, and is now the most segregated part of the whole country.

Fortunately, the solution is obvious. Just mandate integrated schools like before, and leave it to districts to figure out exactly how to get it done. "Which child shall go to what school?" is an inherent question of political power, and rhetoric about reducing government interference or allowing "choice" is in every instance an effort to mask a policy preference requiring the same coercive government power as any other option.

That brings me to housing. Residential segregation does not have the same "advance and retreat" recent history — instead, it's more that we never seriously tried to fix it. Despite the fact that Census data shows most cities have been getting slightly-to-moderately less segregated over the years, it's not remotely enough to actually address the dark legacy of racist housing policy. In most cities with large minority populations, it's still a huge problem.

Obviously, given that neighborhoods change much more slowly than schools, this one isn't so easy. And you wouldn't want to simply bulldoze chunks of Anacostia and slap up luxury towers for upper-class white professionals.

Such is what happened in the case of Breonna Taylor, who was shot eight times during a no-knock raid conducted by the Louisville Metro Police Department on March 13, 2020. Ms. Taylor just so happened to live on the West Side of Louisville, Kentucky, a place well known to locals as a high crime poverty-stricken area. While the police did suspect that Ms. Taylor's apartment was being used as a "drop" for illegal drugs. But there was something possibly more sinister at play here. Because the Louisville

Metro Government had slated the area which Ms. Taylor's house was in an area that they were trying to gentrify. In an amended complaint to their lawsuit, Taylor's lawyers add the claim that Glover himself was unjustly targeted by a special police squad called Place-Based Investigation, because he was one of the "primary roadblocks" to gentrification in the area — the Russell neighborhood of Louisville in which Glover rented his home is part of a multimillion-dollar city revitalization effort called Vision Russell. According to the complaint, Glover was arrested for a second time on April 23. The city then moved to purchase his house, one of several recent foreclosure acquisitions in the area; in June, the city finally acquired it for $17,000. Taylor's attorneys argue that Taylor was included in the search warrant targeted at Glover as part of the trumped-up set of accusations against him, fueled by the city's desire to remove him from the neighborhood. On May 21, the Federal Bureau of Investigation announced it had opened an inquiry into Taylor's death, but so far none of the officers involved in Taylor's death has been arrested or charged with any crime. Louisville police chief Steve Conrad was fired on June 1, after police killed another Black Louisville resident: David McAtee, a local restaurant owner, who was shot to death when police "returned fire" into a group of people gathered outside his restaurant. None of the officers had their body cams turned on.

On June 23, Detective Brett Hankison was notified in a letter by the Louisville Police Department that he had been terminated. "I find your conduct a shock to the conscience," the city's new police chief Robert Schroeder wrote in the letter. "I am alarmed and stunned you used deadly force in this fashion." Lonita Baker, an attorney for the Taylor family, said that they were happy with the development but added, "This is just one step, though ... We're waiting for the other officers to be held accountable and for additional charges to be filed." The two other officers remain on the force.

Nevertheless, there are many ways to chip away at the problem in a sensible and humane fashion. Simply addressing school segregation is probably the best first step, because it removes one major motivation for white flight behavior. Federal housing subsidies of all kinds can be predicated on cities taking meaningful steps to integrate (during the Obama administration, initial steps were taken in this direction, though mainly with low-income subsidies). Indeed, many cities have done some of this of their own volition.

And instead of trying to quickly mix up neighborhoods and thereby risk displacing poorer minorities, cities can keep their affordable housing stock expanding fast enough to prevent displacement, and thereby create neighborhood integration. (For example, from 2001-2011, D.C. lost nearly 40,000 black residents, though it since has started to gain them again.) New housing developments can be incentivized to be demographically and class balanced — particularly social housing, or state-owned apartment buildings for which all residents are eligible; those can be simply required to be integrated.

All that will probably take decades. But given consistent pressure, American neighborhoods can become a satisfying blend of peoples. All it takes is the political will. And given the current nature of the political beast, political will is in short supply. Our elected officials can find all kinds of money for military interventions, but does not have the resources to pay for probably the most important function of our government, that is, educating future generations.

Chapter Six

On weekends, North Smithfield Manor smells like freshly cut grass, as men venture out under the Alabama sun to tend to their lawns. Kids race their bikes up and down the neighborhood's hilly streets. Leslie Williams, a 34-year-old mother of three, lives in her childhood home in this secluded subdivision, perched atop a ridge five miles north of downtown Birmingham. The neighborhood hasn't changed much since Williams was growing up. She remembers riding her bike over the same hills, admiring the men with their lawn mowers, and hanging out in the small park that serves as the community's heart.

After her husband took a job that would keep him on the road most of the time, Williams moved back in with her parents in 2012 to save money. Her daughter, 12, and two sons, 11 and 10, started school, and Williams got a job in medical billing in Jasper, 30 minutes from Birmingham. The plan was for her children to follow in another longtime neighborhood tradition. Since 1971, a county school bus has arrived to take kids from North Smithfield Manor, a small pocket of suburban bliss built by black families who were blocked from buying homes in white subdivisions, to Gardendale High School, Williams's alma mater, eight miles north. But if the white parents in Gardendale get their way, that 46-year-old tradition may come to an end.

On May 16, the eve of the 63rd anniversary of the Supreme Court's landmark Brown v. Board of Education school-segregation decision, Williams saw a post on Facebook shared by an old high-school friend she knew from her days playing trumpet in the Gardendale marching band: The newly empowered Gardendale Board of Education would be meeting in a few hours. Gardendale, a mostly white city 15 minutes north of Birmingham, had proposed separating from the Jefferson County School District, which encompasses Birmingham's suburbs. The majority of children living in Jefferson County's increasingly diverse subdivisions are black and Latino; Gardendale's new district would be about 80 percent white. The move had come to the attention of the federal judge overseeing a decades-old desegregation order that requires Jefferson County—once a front in the resistance against the Brown decision—to maintain racially integrated schools.

Williams knew that she had to be there, so she asked her parents to watch the kids. North Smithfield Manor has long been zoned for Gardendale schools as part of the district's integration efforts, and Williams had planned her life around sending her children to Gardendale High, where more than seven out of 10 graduates enroll in college, one of the highest rates in the district. The majority-white city's secession effort soon turned Williams into a reluctant community spokesperson.

Williams is a woman with a strong, round face and prominent features, and she easily charms strangers with her warmth and wit. That night, she twisted her braided hair into a tight bun and put on black slacks and a black-and-white cardigan, then headed out the door to fight the rush-hour traffic.

When she arrived at Gardendale City Hall, there was only standing room left in the large, mahogany-paneled hearing room. One of just a handful of black attendees, Williams walked past police officers and walls decorated with photos of the suburban city's current and former elected officials, all of whom are white, to take an open spot along the wall. Six years into a parent-led campaign to break off from the Jefferson County School District, the Gardendale school board was meeting to discuss how it would set up the new district. Jefferson County's desegregation order meant that Gardendale had been forced to get permission from the federal courts. Weeks earlier, the federal judge overseeing the case, Madeline Hughes Haikala, had approved the formation of the new school district. Haikala's ruling meant that Gardendale could effectively wall itself off from Jefferson County's schools. With their own separate district, Gardendale schools would be open only to Gardendale residents, instead of the much larger and more diverse swath of Jefferson County that they currently serve. Families in Williams's virtually all-black neighborhood were set to lose access to the schools that have served their community for half a century.

"The media has twisted and turned this issue to make everyone think this is about race." —Chris Orazine, Gardendale parent

After the school board's members discussed their plan for hiring all of the personnel needed to start a new school system in just a few weeks, they opened up the floor to the public. Despite their success in getting their district approved, Gardendale's parents were angry. Over the previous few months, the city's push for a new school district had garnered national attention, including two articles in The Washington Post. "The media has twisted and turned this issue to make everyone think this is about race," said Chris Orazine, a white Gardendale dad. "The people who live in this community and love this community know that nothing is further from the truth. But the fact is that damage has been done."

Speaker after speaker complained about how the city had been portrayed. This wasn't about race, they insisted, but about doing what was best for "our" children. But Williams knew that her children weren't included in that "our." Just the night before, at a meeting in her own neighborhood, Jefferson County's superintendent presented Williams and the other parents with a list of schools their kids could choose if Gardendale left the district. All of the schools served more black and poor students than Gardendale's, and all had far worse test scores. At the Gardendale meeting, Williams stood by quietly until she couldn't take it anymore.

As she headed to the front of the packed hearing room, Williams felt glad that she had dressed up. "I'm a product of the schools they don't want my children to be at," she said later. "I wanted to be a perfect example of why they should include them."

When she got to the front of the room, Williams faced the audience instead of the all-white school board and tried to level with them as parents. "I just want my kids to have the best opportunity, whether it be Jefferson County or whether it be Gardendale," she said. "Like you, I just want my children to have the best.

"The options they've given us are schools that are already overcrowded. I have never had a problem with Gardendale forming their own school system. The problem is: How is this going to be done?"

After the meeting ended, two parents approached Williams in the lobby. One mother tried to convince her that the separation effort had nothing to do with excluding black kids like hers. Looking back, Williams wishes she had made a different argument that night.

"The one thing that would keep my kids off the streets is good education. You are trying to take that from them." —Leslie Williams

"The one thing that would help keep my kids—or any child—off the streets is access to good education," Williams said. "You are trying to take that from them. I don't care how you word it; I don't care how you try to dress it up. The bottom line is you are taking that from them."

I wanted to take a moment to point out the obvious, but one of the speakers made mention of the "our children," when advocating for the creation of a new school district. The speaker denies that it is about race, but once that phrase was spoken, they automatically made it about race. Race and education, it appears, to be the areas in which people feel they can discriminate and get away with it. And then they wonder why Blacks can not find work, are more likely to be incarcerated, and are more likely to repeat the cycle with their children.

Furthermore, I do not, for I consider myself an educated person, understand why people are so offended by having their children attend public schools with peoples from other races and/or cultures? Do they not realize that those values they are attempting to instill in their children, and yes I am speaking directly to the white members of the audience here, will one day be challenged, one day be absolutely decimated by your child discovering that not all Black people are this way, or all Hispanic people are that way? Or is it because you know, as I do, that the days of white people's position as the majority race in this country are numbered, but you are too scared to admit it to them because admitting to them means admitting it to yourself? And worse yet, there is absolutely nothing you can do to stop it. You would figure if you can just keep their educational institutions unequal, white people might still have some shot at power? Trust me, nothing could be further from correct. You see, HBUC's (Historically Black Universities and Colleges,) educate literally thousands of young Black men and women every year. They attend Law and Medical schools and even graduate schools to become teachers, educators and scientists. Any veiled attempt to hold them back ends up backfiring in the end.

Now that is not to say that some Blacks and Hispanics fall through the cracks, just as some white students do. This is mainly because the parents or caregivers do not place enough emphasis on education, for whatever reason that might be. And as a result, we have students who are not motivated to learn in an insufficient environment for learning complicated by both their race and socio-economic status. Unfortunately, their chances of being arrested and becoming part of the prison industrial complex increases exponentially at the point which they decide to become truant or drop out from school altogether.

It's illegal to form a school district with the purpose of excluding people because of their race. Yet over the years, Jefferson County's white residents have been allowed to carve out half a dozen exclusive enclaves. In 1954, when the Supreme Court handed down its landmark Brown ruling declaring that separate schools for black and white children were inherently unequal, there were five school districts in Jefferson County. In the 63 years since then, that number has more than doubled as white communities established new school districts separate from the increasingly black and Latino county district. If Gardendale succeeds, it would become the 13th school district in Jefferson County. While this kind of splintering has been going on across the country, what makes the Jefferson County case unique is the federal government's power to stop it there. That's because Jefferson County is one of just 176 school districts, out of the 13,500 across the nation, that are still under federal oversight to make sure they're keeping their promise to fully eliminate all vestiges of Jim Crow.

Yet six decades after Brown, federal judges and officials rarely check to see if districts are obeying their orders to desegregate—and in many cases, schools in districts with a history of discrimination against black children have actually grown more segregated under federal supervision. And when the judges do step in, they've often sided with the districts where school segregation is getting worse. Leslie Williams and the other parents who have fought these moves have been left wondering how the courts and the Justice Department could have so completely turned their backs on the vision of integrated schools first charted out by civil-rights lawyers and the courts in the 1950s and '60s.

"To separate [African-American children] from others of similar age and qualifications solely because of their race generates a feeling of inferiority as to their status in the community that may affect their hearts and minds in a way unlikely ever to be undone," wrote Chief Justice Earl Warren in his Brown v. Board of Education opinion. Warren cited the work of black psychologists Kenneth and Mamie Clark. The husband-and-wife team used dolls to examine the effects of segregation on black children, finding evidence of internalized racism in the black children's clear preference for the white dolls.

Since then, the focus has turned to academic performance, usually as measured by test scores, and over the years even conservative scholars like Eric Hanushek, a fellow at the Hoover Institution at Stanford University, have found that segregation hurts children of color. Researchers have observed that while the racial test-score gap isn't completely closed when schools are integrated, black students' scores tend to go up when they're in integrated environments. White children's scores, meanwhile, aren't affected either way by exposure to children of color. In his research, Rucker Johnson, an economist at the University of California, Berkeley, has looked beyond test scores. He's found that white students who attend integrated schools have measurably less racial prejudice and tend to live in more integrated neighborhoods as adults. As for African Americans, Johnson has found that those who attended integrated schools earn more as adults, live longer, healthier lives, and even pass down these benefits to their children.

So white children's test scores are NOT affected, either positively or negatively, by exposure to children of color? To hear these parents talk, they think their children's world would end if they had to attend school with one of "those" people. Let's face it, prejudice is born of ignorance, and ignorance can be dealt with by education. However, this borders upon pure racism.

"There are long-term impacts that sometimes test scores don't even pick up," Johnson says. "If you only focus on the educational outcomes, you grossly understate the impact of these court cases." Adult incomes for black children in integrated schools were improved, and "the likelihood of being in poverty, the likelihood of incarceration, were all significantly reduced—and the longer they were exposed to integrated schools, the bigger the payoff."

"We've always had problems with Gardendale. It was a sundown town—blacks didn't even buy gas there." —U.W. Clemon, attorney

In 2001, Williams graduated from Gardendale High and moved to Huntsville to attend Alabama A&M. By the time she returned in 2012, the county district had transformed from one in which white students made up almost 80 percent of the student body to one that primarily serves black and Latino children. The number of students from families with incomes low enough to qualify for federal lunch aid had increased from 27 percent to 56 percent. Every time a white community jettisoned the county district, they left behind an increasingly nonwhite and poorer student body and put more pressure on the remaining white communities to follow suit.

"Segregated environments breed unequal allocation of resources," says Johnson, who is working on a book about school segregation. "We as a nation must come to terms with what segregation does. We have to recognize that it's not just about the ideal of integrating schoolchildren, but about ensuring equal educational opportunities."

When breakaway districts leave, they don't only take students and school buildings with them; they also take tax revenue. The state of affairs in sprawling, diverse Jefferson County is a case in point. In the early 2000s, two cities, Leeds and Trussville, with schools that were 62 and 87 percent white, respectively, left the county district to form their own majority-white school systems. After Trussville broke off in 2005, school officials there set about building the most expensive school ever constructed in Alabama: Hewitt-Trussville High School. The new district's boundary lines are jagged: They include prized retail establishments and exclude modest neighborhoods and rental complexes like the Bentwood Apartments, a set of tidy two-story apartment buildings. The brick buildings are racially integrated, but the majority of families with school-age children are black. While Hewitt-Trussville is the closest public high school to the Bentwood Apartments, its doors are locked to the families there. Instead, Bentwood kids go to a county school that is farther away in the other direction—the very situation that prompted the Brown v. Board of Education decision more than 60 years ago.

The nearby county high school is 66 percent black; Hewitt-Trussville is 81 percent white. Trussville officials did make sure to draw in the shopping malls, though. So when Bentwood residents go up to the main road to spend their money, their sales-tax dollars flow to the very schools they can't use.

When Williams decided to move back to Jefferson County, she inadvertently entered her family into a battle that is likely to be one of the last fronts in the long war for school desegregation. It's a battle that black families and school integrationists are losing.

Gardendale's effort to break off from the Jefferson County School District has proceeded in fits and starts for decades now. According to U.W. Clemon, an attorney who represented black families in Stout v. Jefferson County, the desegregation case that covers Jefferson and all of its splinter districts, people in Gardendale have talked about splitting off since court-mandated desegregation started in 1971. "We've always had problems with Gardendale. It was a sundown town—blacks didn't even buy gas there," says Clemon, who grew up in Jefferson County.

But the idea was taken up in earnest in the 1990s, after the city of Hoover became the first to break away from the Jefferson County district since the early '70s. Scott Beason, a longtime state representative and senator, brought the idea out of Gardendale living rooms when he began talking about the split in the halls of the Capitol in Montgomery. Beason, a Gardendale resident, is one of Alabama's most controversial figures. He was a driving force behind the state's infamous 2011 immigration crackdown, which required police to inquire about the legal status of anyone they had a "reasonable suspicion" was in the country unlawfully. Beason has said that Republican lawmakers need to "empty the clip" on "illegal immigrants" or risk losing the state. In 2011, in a voting-rights case, a federal court found that Beason had displayed outright racial bias, citing, among other examples, the time he called black people "aborigines." His "statements demonstrate a deep-seated racial animus," the judge in the case wrote.

The push for a separate Gardendale district fizzled out after two feasibility studies, the first in 1999 and another in 2005, both recommended against forming a new district. But two local dads revived the idea in 2011. David Salters is a father of four and a sales and operations director at a professional—services firm. Born in Birmingham in 1972, just as white families began fleeing the city in large numbers, Salters has seen the long-lasting impact of white flight. His family moved to Morris, a working-class city in north Jefferson County. Salters graduated from a nearly all-white Mortimer Jordan High in 1991. He says the school wasn't especially good: Less than half of his classmates went on to college after graduation. Salters himself spent 13 years working off and on trying to finish his bachelor's degree. He eventually graduated from the University of Alabama at the age of 31. In his graduation photos, Salters is holding a baby—his oldest son—and posing with his dad, who didn't complete high school. Since then, Salters has spent most of his career working in sales.

Former state senator Scott Beason, a champion of separate school districts, once called black people "aborigines."

Driving around Birmingham on a June afternoon, Salters points out the apartment complexes and neighborhoods that his family once lived in, their streets now pocked with blighted houses. "People will just leave," he says. He's concerned that Gardendale will follow the same path as Center Point, which the mass departure of white families transformed into a majority-black suburb, now home to the district's lowest-performing schools.

Salters is proud that he's come further than his own parents, but he also worries that his kids will struggle as much as he did to earn a degree. In 2011, he and another dad, Chris Lucas, a lawyer at a Birmingham-based bank, began talking about what they perceived as a deterioration in the quality of Gardendale schools. Salters said that he and Lucas, also a graduate of the University of Alabama, were particularly alarmed by the ACT scores. "The average ACT score at Gardendale High School is a 19; the average student entering Alabama has a 26," Salters says. "We're not talking about trying to get our kids into a super-elite school like Vanderbilt or Emory. We're worried that they won't have the opportunities we had."

In September 2012, Tim Bagwell, another dad, set up a Facebook group for Gardendale's latest separation campaign. He added Lucas as an administrator, and Lucas added Salters. By October 2012, they had convinced the City Council to fund the third feasibility study in 13 years. The 2005 study had concluded that the cost of constructing a new high school was one of the barriers to forming a new district; but in the interim, the county had built a brand-new $55 million high school in Gardendale with money the district had raised from a countywide penny sales tax and new debt. The new Gardendale High School added 300,000 square feet to the existing building. The school now hosts a 650-seat performing-arts center, a 100-seat lecture hall, and two gyms: a 1,600-seat competition gym and a 300-seat practice gym. It also has a new baseball stadium, softball stadium, and practice fields.

The new construction had to be approved by all of the parties involved in Jefferson County's desegregation case. Everyone agreed, under the assumption that the school would serve as a regional career and technical- education (CTE) center. As a sort of magnet program, the new school would help Jefferson County's desegregation efforts by drawing students from around the district. Three predominantly white schools, Corner High, Mortimer Jordan High, and Oak Grove High, and two predominantly black schools, Center Point High and Minor High, would send some of their students there for CTE courses. During court testimony, Craig Pouncey, the superintendent of the Jefferson County School District, called the new Gardendale school "the epitome of one of the

best high schools anyone could ever hope for"
and "an asset to any community."

The author of the latest feasibility study—an
expert who had been brought in by other
splinter districts—agreed with that assessment.
If Gardendale could separate and take the high
school with it, the district would boast a brand-
new facility with very little debt, a fact that the
expert called "unprecedented" and "remarkable."
But the expert outlined one major hurdle still
left: To pay for the new district, supporters
would have to get residents in this conservative
community to vote in favor of increasing their
own taxes. A referendum was placed on the
ballot for November 12, 2013.

By then, Salters and the other dads had
formalized the secession effort in an organization
called FOCUS Gardendale, which they
incorporated as a nonprofit to campaign for the
property-tax increase. The group enlisted former
state senator Beason to give them political
advice. While Beason wasn't out front in this
push, he and his wife contributed money to
FOCUS Gardendale, and his former campaign
manager assisted the group.

1954: "Brown v. Board of Education" outlawed
segregation and declared "separate but equal" a
dangerous fiction.

In addition to going door-to-door asking voters to
support the tax, the secession effort's
proponents created a number of campaign ads.

In one flier, they asked voters to consider Gardendale's future. The flier showed a young white girl looking up at the question: "Which path will Gardendale choose?" To her side are two lists of communities in Jefferson County. The first includes towns that have large and growing black populations, all of them still served by the county district. The second list includes "some of the best places to live in the country"; they're the predominantly white cities that formed their own school districts, where the enrollment ranges from 57 to 82 percent white. The supporters also put together a video that laid out the benefits of a new school district and warned against what might happen if Gardendale stayed in the county district. "By voting yes, we eliminate the possibility of our own Gardendale High School becoming a regional school," a voice-over intoned. "By voting yes, we avoid the risk of our local children being negatively impacted by the possible merger of the Jefferson County School Board with the Birmingham City School Board." (At the time, the predominantly black Memphis City schools in Tennessee had just been absorbed into the mostly white county district; subsequently, six majority-white suburbs there formed their own districts.)

The campaigning worked. About 35 percent of Gardendale voters turned out for the special election and voted by a margin of 58–42 to approve the tax. After the vote, the City Council appointed the first members of the new Gardendale Board of Education. By June 2014, they had recruited Patrick Martin as the new superintendent. Martin, whose wife was moving to Birmingham to take a coaching job at the University of Alabama campus there, was recruited from a small district near Peoria, Illinois. When U.W. Clemon, the lawyer in the Stout case, deposed him, Martin testified that he had never hired a black teacher in his life. He had also never worked in a district that was more than 5 percent African-American. It would be Martin's responsibility to come up with a desegregation plan that would have to include, among other things, a strategy for hiring more black teachers.

At the same time, the new Gardendale school board went about negotiating a separation agreement with Jefferson County. When they were unable to agree on terms like a suitable price for the high school, they petitioned the state superintendent to mediate. During that time, Beason tried and failed to enlist the governor's help. Eventually, the state superintendent sided with Gardendale and approved the split, but noted that the federal court overseeing Jefferson County's desegregation case would have the final say.

David Salters says this was the first time that Jefferson Country had invoked the desegregation case. He thinks that county officials triggered the case as their last, best hope to keep

Gardendale's $55 million high school in the district. At the time, Salters didn't think the desegregation case would be a barrier, because he and the other Gardendale parents had seen so many other cities leave county districts that were still under court order. In addition to Leeds and Trussville in Jefferson County, Pelham and Alabaster—two Birmingham suburbs in neighboring Shelby County—had recently been allowed to break away. Salters wonders where the NAACP's Legal Defense Fund, the Justice Department, and the federal courts were when those splits happened uneventfully. Indeed, the Justice Department had given its blessing in all those cases, and the NAACP Legal Defense Fund even sided with Leeds and Trussville. But that was before U.W. Clemon returned to the case and breathed new life into the county's desegregation fight.

In its first court filings, Gardendale implied that the Supreme Court's Brown ruling was now outdated. The city's lawyers urged the judge to rely on decisions that the Supreme Court had made since 1991, when the Court, under Chief Justice William Rehnquist, had started chipping away at Brown's legacy. Gardendale also cited Shelby County v. Holder, a case that originated in another Birmingham suburb that eventually led the Court to gut the Voting Rights Act in 2012. Gardendale argued that "courts must open their eyes to the conditions of the present when they consider" the degree to which court-ordered consent decrees impinge "on federalism and the Tenth Amendment."

The assertion that the county's current desegregation order, which was finalized in 1971, had become antiquated provoked a strong reaction from Judge Haikala.

"The Supreme Court's holding in Brown is simple and unaffected by the passage of time: when black public-school students are treated as if they are inferior to white students, and that treatment is institutionalized by state or municipal action, the resulting stigma unconstitutionally assails the integrity of black students. That racial stigma is intolerable under the Fourteenth Amendment. That was true in 1954, and it is true today," she wrote. "For black children who waited until 1865 to be recognized as United States citizens [with the ratification of the 13th Amendment] and then waited until 1971 to be admitted into white classrooms in Jefferson County public schools, the 46-year-old desegregation order in this case must seem relatively young."

In contrast to the cases of Trussville and Leeds, when the Justice Department under George W. Bush stood on the sidelines, Barack Obama's Justice Department came out against Gardendale leaving Jefferson County. Federal lawyers filed a brief calling for the courts to block the separation. Amy Berman, who worked on these cases under both the Bush and Obama administrations, says the Justice Department has actively opposed several of these splinter districts but has been unable to sway the courts, which make the final decision on them.

Meanwhile, Clemon rounded up new plaintiffs for Jefferson County's old desegregation case, mostly parents and grandparents from North Smithfield Manor, Leslie Williams's neighborhood. Clemon, who grew up attending all-black Jefferson County schools, started fighting splinter districts after he graduated from Columbia Law School in 1968 and the NAACP Legal Defense Fund assigned him to Jefferson County. He was on the case until 1980, when President Jimmy Carter appointed him as a federal judge. Gardendale's push to separate from the Jefferson County School District brought Clemon out of retirement, because he thinks it could prove to be a dangerous precedent.

"If Gardendale is successful," Clemon says, "every other majority-white community that wishes to withdraw from a metro system under [court] order can do so."

The South's schools were once the most integrated in the country, thanks to the heavy hand of the federal government as it tried to force Southern districts to abide by Brown v. Board of Education. From 1968 to 1980, during the height of aggressive court supervision, the number of black students attending highly segregated schools in the South fell from almost 80 percent to a low of about 23 percent. But in the last three and a half decades, the number of black students attending segregated schools in the South has increased to nearly 36 percent. The federal government's retreat is a main factor in the return of segregated schooling in the South. In 2000, there were 430 school districts under federal court order to desegregate, compared with 176 today. Without the feds watching, local school boards are prone to make decisions that end up separating kids by race.

Even in places where the federal government is supposed to be paying attention, segregation is on the rise. Most of the 176 districts still under supervision are in the Deep South, the result of whole swaths of Alabama, Mississippi, and Georgia being put under supervision in statewide cases. But the rest are scattered across the United States and include places like Tucson, Arizona, and Waterbury, Connecticut. Out of that total, 69 have a student body diverse enough to run integrated schools, but local officials instead chose to operate "racially identifiable" or segregated campuses, according to a Hechinger Report analysis of enrollment data.

Alabama is home to the most students attending school districts under federal supervision, and these schools follow the national pattern. In 1995, the first year of readily available enrollment data in Alabama, 10 out of the 40 districts under continuous court supervision had demographics that would have allowed them to integrate, but instead chose to run 48 segregated schools. Today, 12 districts that could integrate run 101 segregated schools that serve just over 54,000 children—an increase of almost 30,000 students.

Last year, the Government Accountability Office issued a scathing report chiding the Justice Department for not even tracking basic details about the districts that remain under order. In 2014, Madeline Hughes Haikala, the judge overseeing many of the remaining desegregation cases in northern Alabama, including Gardendale's, came to a similar conclusion while reviewing Huntsville's 40-year-old desegregation case.

"From the record, it appears that years of relative calm and inactivity have lulled the government into a habit of checking in only when the district proposes actions that require the government's review," Haikala wrote. "Based on the current record, the Court does not know when inequities in educational programs arose in the district; however, standardized test scores from 10 years ago demonstrate disparate results among racially identifiable schools. Had the government been keeping an eye on that sort of information, it could have brought it to the Court's attention more quickly and enabled the Court and the district to address the issue in a timely fashion."

The South's schools were once the most integrated in the country, thanks to the heavy hand of the federal government.

Former Justice Department lawyers defend the department's work, saying that both Democratic and Republican administrations have failed to adequately invest in making desegregation real. While Obama's Justice Department racked up wins in dozens of cases, including a high-profile case in Cleveland, Mississippi, officials in many districts with segregated schools report that they hadn't heard from either the Justice Department or the courts during Obama's tenure.

Many of the 176 outstanding cases have been in a state of suspended animation for years, if not decades. While the original court-mandated desegregation plans usually required districts to provide reports on a semi-annual basis, many districts don't bother. Officials in several districts contacted by The Hechinger Report said that they hadn't heard from the Justice Department or the courts in 20 years.

One former high-level figure in Obama's Justice Department said that during the federal hiring freeze that took hold in 2011, the department's Educational Opportunities Section, which not only oversees all of the school-desegregation cases but also other cases involving equal access to quality education, had only a dozen or so lawyers handling the section's 350 cases. (The

Justice Department declined to confirm the number of cases.) According to one former official from Obama's Justice Department, it simply didn't have the manpower to actively oversee every district still under order, so it relied instead on community members and activists on the ground to bring the department's attention to problem spots. That strategy put the onus to fight for integrated schools on some of the country's most historically marginalized communities.

Lawyers inside and outside of the Justice Department say the department's attorneys must be cautious. Over the last two decades, judges and case law have become increasingly hostile to those seeking to compel districts to desegregate their schools. The precedent was set in 1991, when the Supreme Court ruled in the case of Board of Education of Oklahoma City v. Dowell that lower-court judges should dissolve desegregation plans if they believed that the districts had accomplished as much integration as was feasible. That ruling has provided an easy out for many districts. Since 2000, more than 250 districts overseen by the Justice Department have been declared "unitary," meaning they've done all that's "feasible" to eliminate their Jim Crow systems, leaving the Justice Department almost no power to tackle inequalities in those communities.

"There's never been more than a very small handful of lawyers that have been working on these cases," says Gary Orfield, a desegregation scholar who has served as an expert witness in desegregation cases since the 1970s. "There's no one who can go to Two Springs, Mississippi, to check out what's going on. In American law in general, nothing happens unless someone files an order. The problem is you have school districts and courts that were never enthusiastic about this. I just talked to a district that didn't know they were under court order. There may have been 10 superintendents since this all started."

The next few years may well prove to be the last in the federal effort to desegregate schools. Trump's presidency could provide the final blow. During George W. Bush's administration, almost 200 districts shed their court orders. With just 176 districts left, Trump's Justice Department could bring an end to the 63-year-old effort to erase the legacy of Jim Crow in the American education system, at a time when nearly 8.4 million black and Latino children are learning in segregated and high-poverty schools.

The Justice Department failed to respond to multiple requests for comment.

Leslie Williams says she's torn about all of this. Before going to Gardendale High School, she attended an all-black Christian school run by a neighbor. She doesn't think there's necessarily anything wrong with an all-black school, but she would like her three children to be exposed to people from different kinds of backgrounds, just as she was at Gardendale High—the kind of education that is quickly disappearing across the South. Williams wants them to be in a place where they won't feel pressure to fit into any box—where her daughter, who plays alto saxophone, her sports-loving middle son, and her science-loving younger son can explore their interests.

"I want to say, 'Of course diversity is a good thing,' but it's a blessing and a curse," Williams says. "The blessing is, you get to be around different groups of people, you are learning different things—but the problem is, not all groups are as welcoming to the idea of being inclusive and being diverse. Some people are only forced to be around other people."

After the desegregation issue was raised, Gardendale had to change course. The district as originally proposed was intended only for Gardendale residents, but once desegregation came up, the organizers decided to add students from North Smithfield Manor. In new court filings, the district proposed allowing them to attend school there "indefinitely," although the mostly black suburb wouldn't be formally included in the district's boundaries. Legally, Gardendale can't annex North Smithfield Manor and make it part of the city, because the two communities aren't contiguous. So the arrangement would be tenuous. North Smithfield Manor parents couldn't vote in school-board elections and wouldn't have a say in how the district was run. And when Gardendale's desegregation order is dissolved, nothing would stop the district from dropping the neighborhood.

This proposed arrangement didn't satisfy Judge Haikala. "Race was a motivating factor in Gardendale's decision to separate from the Jefferson County public school system," Haikala wrote in April 2017. "More specif-ically, a desire to control the racial demographics of the four public schools in the City of Gardendale and the racial demographics of the city itself motivated the grassroots effort to separate and to eliminate from the Gardendale school zone black students whom Jefferson County transports to Gardendale schools under the terms of the desegregation order."

Haikala supported her contention that race was driving the secession effort with quotes from several of David Salters's Facebook posts. "A look around at our community sporting events, our churches are great snapshots of our community," Salters wrote. "A look into our schools, and you'll see something totally different." In another post, he wrote: "We are using buses to transport nonresidents into our schools (without additional funding) from as far away as Center Point (there's your redistribution of wealth)."

Salters insists that his Facebook posts were taken out of context and that his campaign to create a new school district was driven by his desire to improve the quality of education, rather than to exclude children from outside of Gardendale. He adds that residents in the conservative community wouldn't have voted to increase their taxes if they didn't think there were real problems with how the schools were being run.

Haikala, an Obama appointee, has been tougher on school districts than almost any judge in decades. But in the end, that didn't mean much. In April, she ruled that Gardendale could break away. Gardendale would start with two elementary schools and would have to work in "good faith" to earn the middle and high schools. She also eliminated from the proposed new district North Smithfield Manor and the other outlying white communities, which would have enjoyed a 13-year grandfathering period, arguing that this only created more uncertainty for Jefferson County's desegregation efforts. Haikala said she ultimately sided with Gardendale because she understood the merits of local control and because she feared that black kids in Gardendale would be targeted if she ruled against the white residents.

"Years of relative calm have lulled the government into checking in only when the district proposes actions that require review." — Judge Madeline Hughes Haikala

But the alternative may prove worse for black families. When Leslie Williams moved back to North Smithfield Manor in 2012, it was a good bet: The Gardendale schools have served families from North Smithfield relatively well. According to a report done by the Justice Department's education expert, Gardendale High enrolls more of its black students in Advanced Placement courses than the three high schools where North Smithfield Manor families may eventually end up sending their children. At Gardendale, which offers 12 AP classes, a quarter of black students enroll in at least one of those courses. Fultondale High and Center Point High, where North Smithfield Manor students could be transferred, offer only six AP courses, and just 8 percent of black students enroll in them. Indeed, the majority of Center Point students who go on to attend an Alabama public college have to take remedial courses to catch up to their peers.

Both Gardendale and the black families contesting its secession effort have filed appeals, which means Gardendale city schools won't start up this fall as planned. The Justice Department, now led by Trump appointee Jeff Sessions, has yet to weigh in on the case.

Few places under the Justice Department's watch have been as bold as Gardendale. In the other 175 districts under court order to desegregate, the process of abandoning Brown's mandate has been much quieter and more complicated, if no less harmful to the students living there. Pickens County, Alabama, a rural school district 80 miles west of Birmingham, is one of those places still on the Justice Department's docket where integration has eroded slowly, with little notice from the feds.

Pickens County forms the northern tip of the Alabama Black Belt, a reference both to the dark, fertile soils that once supported a thriving cotton-plantation economy and to the people who live there. To this day, the county is home to far more black residents than communities just to the north, which are nearly all-white. Today, timberland accounts for most of the county's acreage, and trucks stacked with freshly cut logs roar up and down the county's two-lane highways. Pickens County is also home to over 500 working farms, and together agriculture and forestry provide nearly half of the jobs. Little has changed there in the last half-century, except for the schools.

Pickens County was drawn into a statewide lawsuit responding to Governor George Wallace's notorious campaign to keep black and white students segregated. Black plaintiffs in Macon County, Alabama, won a federal court case that allowed black students to be admitted to the all-white Tuskegee High School in 1963; in response, Wallace sent the National Guard to block the school's doors. When that plan failed, he ordered that Tuskegee High be closed and white parents reimbursed for sending their children to a new all-white private school. Wallace's plan backfired: By so blatantly using the state government to keep schools segregated, he opened the door for Alabama to become the only state in which all public schools had to submit to federal supervision. Alabama districts that weren't already under their own desegregation orders became defendants in the Lee v. Macon case.

At first, Pickens County tried a so-called freedom-of-choice plan, in which families could choose a different school from the one their child attended. During the first year of court-ordered desegregation, the 1967–68 school year, fewer than 1 percent of the county's black students chose to move to one of the white schools. By the 1969–70 school year, 16 percent of black children attended those schools, yet not a single white family had chosen to leave a historically white campus. In 1968, the Supreme Court ruled that choice plans didn't fulfill the promise of Brown. Districts across the country were forced to devise new plans for meaningful integration. In 1969, a federal court finalized a new plan for Pickens County, forcing it to merge its dual system of white and black schools. At the time, the district was 54 percent black. The court created four sets of schools. Under the court's original plan, the demographics of each cluster ranged from 25 percent black, in Gordo, to 72 percent black, in Aliceville. But in the last couple of decades, the schools in Pickens County have become increasingly segregated.

From the beginning, Pickens County officials undermined the new desegregation plan. For decades, they allowed white students zoned to majority-black schools to quietly transfer to other schools both inside and outside the county. In 1989, black residents of Pickens County sidestepped the Justice Department and filed a complaint with the US Department of Education's Office for Civil Rights. The office found that the district had indeed been using transfers to allow white students to escape majority-black schools. While the district didn't admit to improper transfers, it agreed to tighten up its transfer policies. A 1994 court agreement required Pickens County to deny transfer requests that would hinder desegregation efforts, although there were a number of exceptions—for example, families could get a transfer if they established that a school placement jeopardized a child's health or safety.

But the rampant transfers continued unabated. In 1998, in its reports to the court, the district acknowledged granting 123 transfers that year. A third of those transfers were for white students to leave Aliceville schools, where just six white students remained. The pattern continued for years, until the Justice Department reached out to the district in the early 2000s. But by 2003, the damage had already been done. In Carrollton, the small county seat, the elementary and high schools so struggled to keep up white enrollment that in 2006, Pickens County asked the Justice Department and the federal courts to let it close all of the town's schools. The Justice Department sided with county officials. In justifying their decision, the department's lawyers made a point of noting that a black superintendent introduced the plan to close the predominantly black schools.

Today, the remaining schools in Pickens County are a picture of the half-hearted progress that the nation has made toward ending its legacy of racial segregation. Two schools in the county remain integrated: In the town of Reform, an elementary school and high school have student populations that are close to the overall makeup of the district. But over 80 percent of the district's white students attend Gordo schools, where white students make up 64 percent of the population. More than half of the district's black students go to school in Aliceville, where black students comprise 98 percent of the student body.

Similarly, across the 176 school districts still under order, black and Latino students are increasingly enrolled in schools that don't reflect their district's racial makeup. When demographics in a school vary from the district's overall numbers by more than 20 percentage points—for example, a school that is 60 percent black in a district that's only 35 percent black—

experts call these schools "racially identifiable." They say these numbers signal that a district could do more to integrate. In Pickens County, five out of the seven schools are racially identifiable. And looking at all of the 40 Alabama districts the federal government has been overseeing for decades, there are 125 racially identifiable schools today, up from 72 in 1995. Today, almost 64,000 Alabama children attend such schools, despite being enrolled in districts under court order to desegregate.

While there was talk in the early 1990s about consolidating Pickens County schools—two of the county's three high schools serve just about 275 kids, and Gordo serves 550 students—that idea was quickly quashed by vocal opposition from white parents in Gordo. No one believes that integration is really a possibility in Pickens County anymore, despite the desegregation order that's supposed to dictate how schools are run in the district. Instead, officials and many local residents are all in agreement that the focus should be on improving the quality of education for black students. The court approved a new "desegregation" plan in 2011. It focuses on eliminating disparities between black and white students in a variety of areas, including graduation rates, suspensions and exclusions, scholarships, and enrollment in advanced courses like honors and AP classes.

"Race was a motivating factor in Gardendale's decision to separate from the Jefferson County public school system." —Judge Haikala

Vanessa Anthony, the district's associate superintendent and a graduate of Aliceville High School, thinks Lee v. Macon helped the district. "Like with No Child Left Behind forcing us to report out how different groups were doing, the Lee v. Macon case has forced us to look at how everyone is doing, not just the top performers," says Anthony, who is black.

But she also notes that Pickens County has bigger concerns than making sure students are evenly distributed by race across the district's schools. It's hard to get teachers to stay in a rural district with few amenities, and students are moving away too, making it difficult to provide a high-quality education for anyone, Anthony says.

In the end, school officials in Pickens County are hoping they will somehow be able to make separate equal.

So far, however, making separate equal isn't working out very well in the segregated schools that the Justice Department oversees in Alabama and elsewhere. Alabama's data show a relatively strong correlation between segregation and failure, and between integration and success.

In Clinton, Mississippi, a suburb of Jackson, the public schools are 53 percent black and 39 percent white. In response to a desegregation order, the district reconfigured its schools to provide a single school for kindergarten and first grade, another for second and third grade, and so on. The plan allows the district's students to attend school together, ensuring that each school reflects the district's overall racial and socioeconomic makeup. Over the years, even as poverty has increased in the district, the schools have continued to serve both black and white students well. Though there's still a gap in performance between the two groups, Clinton is the only majority-black school district in Mississippi that gets an A on the state's rating system.

Erica Frankenberg, an education professor at Pennsylvania State University, says that integration has a proven track record, but that the fight for securing and maintaining integrated schools has taken a toll even on some of its fiercest proponents.

"You can understand why even some civil-rights lawyers say, 'I'm tired of fighting—I just want the best I can get for the students here,'" Frankenberg says. "But in a lot of these cases, if different decisions would have been made and if the courts had intervened 20 or 30 years ago, the demographics of the schools would have been different. The political lift would have been lighter."

Amy Berman started at the Justice Department in 2002 and spent nine years working on school—desegregation cases under the administrations of both George W. Bush and Barack Obama. After Bush took office, the department began a comprehensive review of its 430-remaining school—desegregation cases, planning to lift orders in as many districts as possible. During that period, federal courts closed out almost 200 cases, including in places like Vestavia Hills, Alabama, where the immediate impact was a return to segregated schools after the district dropped the black neighborhood it had been forced to serve. According to Berman, the approach was starkly different under Obama. While she says the career attorneys working under both administrations often fought vigorously against resegregation, Berman admits that there was a shift in policy under Obama. Rather than helping the districts that requested to dissolve their cases, the Obama administration imposed consent decrees, which required these districts to lay out a plan to address, under court supervision, the lingering disparities between black and white students. This summer, the Justice Department under President Trump reversed course from the Obama administration's policy and said that it would allow Franklin County, Mississippi, to end its court supervision without a consent decree.

With Trump in office, it's probably only a matter of time before the number of federal desegregation orders drops again, possibly to zero. Trump's team is opposed to using consent decrees to keep the pressure on school districts and make sure they've fulfilled their promise to erase the legacy of Jim Crow, arguing that the courts and the Justice Department need to get out of these local matters. Berman and other civil-rights lawyers say they've already heard rumors of districts gearing up to ask the courts to lift their orders, assuming the Trump administration won't fight them.

Meanwhile, the resegregation of the South could soon accelerate. Both Alabama and Mississippi, which together are home to nearly half of the remaining cases, have recently passed laws allowing for charter schools. Frankenberg and other researchers have found that charters tend to increase segregation. The case of Mitchell County, Georgia, is a cautionary tale. In the late 1990s, a group of white residents in Mitchell County used Georgia's nascent charter law to start a new school, which opened in 2000. Once that happened, white families peeled off from the nearly all-black district schools to which they were zoned and enrolled at the Baconton Community Charter School. The federal court overseeing Mitchell County's still-active school-desegregation order didn't interfere. While diversity has increased significantly at Baconton since then, the charter school is still 74 percent white, while the district schools are only 8 percent white. "We have 26 percent students of color, and we do have a plan in place to attract more students of color," said Baconton assistant principal Mary Sullivan in an e-mail.

The final retreat of the federal government from its responsibility to enforce the Brown decision will send a clear message to places like Gardendale. "If you can create a school system with racially inspired motivations, there is nothing stopping the return of segregation," says U.W. Clemon, the civil-rights attorney and former judge.

Leslie Williams isn't optimistic. She's enrolling her second child at the middle school in Gardendale this fall, but she knows the rug could be pulled out from under her at any time. "From education to law enforcement, everything is a struggle for black families," Williams says on a steamy summer afternoon as she weighs her options. "We have to teach our kids to play a game that is set up against them from the beginning."

Chapter Seven

Fifty years ago, the Kerner Commission, appointed by President Lyndon Johnson, issued a seminal report that highlighted racial disparities in America. A half-century later, striking disparities in opportunity—too often drawn along lines of race and class—still exist throughout our nation.

It is important to note that these disparities are a reflection of choices that we have made as a society: As a nation, we are not acting on what we know is in the best interest of our children.

Researchers point to the nation's "double segregation" in which, in community after community, low-income students and students of color are consistently concentrated in a subset of schools, and then those schools are systematically and significantly under-resourced.

This segregation is evident in our nation's capital, where a public school with 11% low-income students and another public school with nearly all low-income students are only 1 mile apart. And in New York City, where I grew up, which is home to 4 million White residents, a Latinx high school student may not encounter White classmates until she goes to college.

A high-quality, well-rounded education, one that includes mathematics and reading as well as the sciences, social studies and civics, world languages, physical education, and the arts, prepares our children to thrive in college and careers, and as engaged members of our democratic society. And yet, students of color and students from low-income families continuously are denied their right to learn because we choose, as a society, to provide them with less.

Gaps in access remain, with students of color and low-income students disproportionately likely to attend a school in which Advanced Placement and International Baccalaureate courses and even subjects such as Chemistry, Physics, and Algebra II are not offered.

According to the latest release from the Civil Rights Data Collection, while 50% of all American high schools offer calculus, just 38% of high schools with high enrollments of Black and Latinx students do so. Certainly, it is unacceptable that just half of our high schools offer calculus; it is also deeply troubling that the vast majority of high schools serving large percentages of students of color do not provide this core course.

We also know from a wealth of research that quality preschool is critical to a child's development. Yet, our most vulnerable children far too often arrive at kindergarten

underprepared to thrive because we provide
them with less access to robust early learning
programs.

Reams of research and years of experience show
that students succeed when they learn in
schools with strong teachers and leaders. Yet,
historically underserved students are far more
likely to attend schools with novice or less
effective teachers.

We also understand the vital, positive impact
that school counselors make on the lives of our
youth, yet too often students of color and
students from low-income communities are
provided with little access to the necessary
social-emotional and college planning supports
that school counselors provide. In fact, 1.6
million students across the country attend a
school where there is a sworn law enforcement
officer and no school counselor. It's hard to
ignore the underlying message about our values
that this sends to our youth, particularly youth
in under-resourced communities.

Finally, we know that students who frequently
miss school will have trouble succeeding
academically. While exclusionary discipline
practices—including suspensions and
expulsions, which take students out of the
learning environment—are declining across
America, there are disturbing
disproportionalities in school discipline
nationwide. Black male students, for example,

represent 8% of all k–12 students, yet they account for a quarter of students who receive one or more out-of-school suspensions.

Time to be up front and honest here. We have failed as a society when it comes to providing a quality education to ALL students, but especially Black, Latino, and Native American students. Our biases and prejudices have led to this problem, so it is no one's fault but our own, and we are the only one's who can fix it. Why? Because we owe a decent education to all children, not just the ones we see as racially pure like white people. Education is the one tool that in our society can be used to move up the socio-economic ladder, maybe that is why we reason that if we give a certain percentage of the population a substandard education, we are guaranteed some form of servitude from certain minorities.

This is a middle-aged white male talking here, whose genetic ancestry is whiter than sour cream, and if I can see the disparages, just think what a Black, Hispanic, or Native American can see. You just have to go back two generations in my family to see blatant racism, My grandfather, who in my youth I idolized, was such a racist. He was raised just a poor farm boy in Eastern Kentucky, but somehow, he thought that due to the color of his skin, made him better than any Black person. He would drop the "N" word about as much as I drop the "F" bomb in my writings. Do I hold it against him? Not really. Because the

man was born in 1916, the height of the Jim
Crow era, also he lived through the Great
Depression, also Jim Crow influenced. For all
but the last 18 years of his life, everything in his
life was segregated. He passed away from Cancer
in 1982 at the age of 65. I often wonder what he
would think of the United States in 2020. Of the
world his grandchildren, great-grandchildren,
and great-great grandchildren are now living in,
some having friends of different races. It is an
interesting thought experiment.

So why is it white people? Why is it you are so
afraid of people whose skin is two shades darker
than a paper sack? C'mon you can admit it to
me, I don't judge people. It's not just Blacks you
fear, it's Hispanics, it's Muslims, It's Asians and
Pacific Islanders. Hell, people in this country
even are afraid of Puerto Ricans even though
they have been citizens of these United States
since 1917! Why, because they have a different
skin color, speak a different language, and have
a different culture then we do. But the obvious
source of all the discrimination has been skin
color. We make assumptions based on skin
color, Back during the Jim Crow era, laws were
passed to protect the "sanctity of white women
from the Negros," and that kiddies is why both
cocaine, heroin, and marijuana were all made
illegal. Cocaine and Heroin because according to
the "medical experts" of the time it made white
women want to associate themselves with Black
men in "jazz clubs." Marijuana was more of a

move against the Hispanic people, this way the white powers that be could not only use law enforcement and the courts to sow fear among those communities, but also get free labor in their prison systems due to a loophole in the 13th amendment, the amendment outlawing slavery. In a later Chapter, we'll examine the school to prison pipeline, and how it is heavily tilted towards minorities.

While it is important for our society to grapple with the reality of what we aren't doing, it is also crucial for us to learn from the places that are choosing to provide equitable educational opportunities to students.

Consider the choices that leaders in Montgomery County, MD are making to ensure meaningful school diversity. The county operates the nation's oldest and largest inclusionary zoning program, a policy that ensures mixed-income housing. That's a choice rooted in the understanding that housing and education are inextricably linked. The county also has an extensive public-school choice program designed in a way that substantially increases diversity in school enrollment.

Montgomery County demonstrates that students who go to diverse schools can perform better over time than students who attend schools in areas of concentrated poverty. In fact, a recent study of the county's housing policy highlights the interconnectedness of inclusionary zoning policies and academic performance. Through random assignment, researchers tracked the performance of elementary students in the county, including those in its inclusionary zoning housing units. The study found that by the end of elementary school, initial achievement gaps between affluent students and the low-income students who attended schools with less poverty were cut by half in mathematics and by one third in reading. And the presence of children from low-income families in the more advantaged schools did not negatively impact the academic performance of the more affluent students.

The reality is that diversity matters, and when districts are intentional about policy levers to advance school diversity, students succeed.

Other initiatives, such as dual-language programs, magnet arts and science, technology, engineering and mathematics (STEM) schools, and regional career and technical high schools, also are proving to be powerful tools in increasing socioeconomic and racial diversity in schools, as well as in reducing achievement gaps.

Consider North Carolina, one of the earlier adopters of dual-language immersion programs. A study found that African American students enrolled in "two-way" dual-language programs significantly outscored their peers who did not participate in the dual-language programs on the state's reading and math tests.

When students attend diverse schools, it can increase empathy, improve their problem-solving skills, and contribute to positive academic outcomes, especially for students from low-income families and students of color. Given the re-segregation of our schools and our current national climate, it is perhaps more critical than ever to ensure that diversity and integration are priorities in our public schools. Diverse schools also must include diverse educators.

Research shows that students of color do better when they have access to diverse teachers and school leaders. In fact, one recent study shows that Black students from low-income families are more likely to graduate from high school and to consider enrolling in college if they are taught by just one Black teacher in elementary school. To be sure, students of color and all students benefit when they are taught by diverse educators who represent a variety of backgrounds, perspectives, and experiences. Indeed, it is important for White students to see teachers and leaders of color in their classrooms and schools.

It's also important to recognize that while diversity at the schoolhouse door is important, it's not good enough. We must make sure that students have a diverse curricular experience and that individual courses—especially those that are most rigorous—are not segregated by race or class. As a nation, we need to recommit to changing our public policies to produce integrated schools.

If education is liberation, then it's our job to knock down barriers and make sure that we are getting every student the educational opportunities that he or she deserves. We can't let another 50 years go by and let down another generation of students. Our kids can't wait. Our future as a nation is at stake.

The extent of racial isolation in the South was far greater than in the North, mainly because of de jure segregation in the South.

Racial imbalance also existed in Northern cities during the mid-1960s, but racial isolation was not nearly so extensive. Most Northern school segregation at that time was thought to be de facto, that is, brought about by the private decisions of citizens to live in different geographic areas. The highest levels of racial isolation existed in Chicago, Cleveland, Detroit, Indianapolis, Milwaukee, and Philadelphia where the black population swelled from post–World War II migration of Southern blacks looking for jobs in the large urban centers of the North. This migration overwhelmed the capacity of white neighborhoods to absorb blacks and still remain integrated, although none but Chicago approached school racial isolation rates of 90 percent. Other large cities with sizable, but in some cases smaller, black enrollments such as Boston, Cincinnati, Columbus (Ohio), Los Angeles, Newark, New York, and San Francisco had no more than half of their black students in predominately black schools.

Chapter Eight

School segregation intensified through the 1990s, during which time three major Supreme Court decisions authorized a return to segregated neighborhood schools. Though the U.S. South is much more integrated now than before the civil rights revolution, it is moving backward. This report describes the background of school resegregation; public opinion and trends in school segregation; benefits of desegregation; costs of segregation; public opinion about desegregation; the effectiveness of strategies for equalizing separate education; the impacts of inferior education; and reasons for returning to segregation. Although student diversity has increased significantly, most children experience separate societies and schools. White children attend more segregated schools than any other racial group. Segregation follows Black and Hispanic families as they move from the city to suburbia. The high level of suburban segregation reported for Black and Hispanic students in this report suggests that a major set of challenges to the future of the minority middle class and to the integration of suburbia need to be addressed. Hispanic children have been more segregated than Blacks for a number of years, not only by race and ethnicity but also by poverty. There is also serious segregation developing by language.

Segregated schools are highly unequal. Segregation by race relates to segregation by poverty and many forms of educational inequality for minority students. Americans believe their children benefit from integrated education, and segregation has not been an effective policy. Segregated schools have significantly higher dropout levels and poorer records of preparing students for higher education. Eleven recommendations are presented, including: expanding the federal magnet school program and imposing desegregation requirements for federally supported charter schools; exploring school and housing policies to avoid massive resegregation of large sections of the inner suburbs; promoting and funding teacher exchanges between city and suburban school districts and training teachers in techniques for successful interracial classrooms; and creating more two-way integrated bilingual schools.

The South went from the most segregated, absolute apartheid region of the country, to the most integrated region of the country, because of federal court orders. And really, from the span of 1964 to the early '70s, you saw a complete transformation of the South, where 90 percent of black students were attending schools with white children, and it was because of those court orders.

But what we found is that there was a heavy enforcement of those court orders for a couple of decades. And then what has resulted has been really non-enforcement of most of these court orders for recent decades.

And that's for a couple of reasons. The Supreme Court has really backed away from desegregation, it hasn't ruled in favor of desegregation for decades, and it made it clear that these desegregation orders were not to be permanent, and that they should end as quickly as possible. Just a real lack of oversight and, I think, political will to enforce the orders. There are dozens of districts where they remained under federal desegregation order, but district leadership didn't know the orders were open, they didn't know what the order said. The DOJ wasn't enforcing. The Department of Ed wasn't enforcing. And they just were sitting dormant, even though students have rights under these orders. The Justice Department isn't even sure what the number of orders is, and their list looks like it might be incomplete, it's really troubling.

It's hard to understand schools and school segregation without understanding housing policy and housing discrimination. I was struck by a line in your piece about school district officials saying there was really not much they could do about the transformation in Tuscaloosa creating an all-black high school, because "you can't help where people live." How does housing discrimination—this is something you've written about extensively, prior to this series—how does that factor into the story of school segregation?

First let me say that in Tuscaloosa, and actually in many districts, that argument that schools are segregated because neighborhoods are segregated wasn't necessarily true for all schools, particularly the high school. There was a great deal of gerrymandering of attendance zones in Tuscaloosa, which we show through mapping. The neighborhood that the all-black high school is located in was a majority white neighborhood, but those kids were bussed to a more integrated school.

But more generally, housing of course drives segregated schools. If you place schools in neighborhoods that are heavily one race or another, you're going to have segregated schools. And in cities like Detroit, and cities like Chicago, New York, of course these are some of the most segregated cities residentially, and so they are also some of the most segregated cities in terms of schools.

And that's part of what the Supreme Court in the early '70s, when it authorized bussing as a form of desegregation in the Charlotte schools, was trying to break that link between housing and schools, understanding that they actually drive each other. If a neighborhood has a segregated school, people who have choices won't move into that neighborhood. And vice versa, if a neighborhood has a stably integrated school, people will tend to move into a neighborhood like that. We often blame residential segregation on school segregation, but the inverse is also true. And that's what subsequent rulings on bussing were trying to break up: that you couldn't buy into an integrated neighborhood, because you may not be going to the school in your neighborhood.

I tell the story through three generations of one family in Tuscaloosa, and the grandfather, even though he started school the year that Brown was decided, he never attended an integrated school. And the only one in the three generations who did attend an integrated school was the mother, who was that kind of in-between generation, when there was real integration. And now her own child is back in segregated schools. I thought that was important, just to lay that history out for Americans, so that we can understand why we are as we are.

But also, of course, hoping that if people are knowledgeable that this is intentional in many ways, that the segregation is not accidental, because we've also let ourselves off the hook as a society, because we believe in the inevitability of all of this, or that it's somehow a benign process that leads to schools being 99 percent black and Latino, I wanted to show very clearly that it's not, and that reporters can dig in their own communities, and look at the policy decisions that have led to the resegregation.

And thirdly, on a very small scale, in Tuscaloosa, I knew there had long been people who believed that deals had been made, but could never prove it. And in Tuscaloosa, there are conversations that have not happened before, there's proof that the community didn't have before. And as that community is getting ready to redistrict its schools yet again, the conversation there is very different. They know that someone's watching, and the people who want more equity now feel like they have the power to push for it.

The language of the Court's unanimous decision in Brown was groundbreaking, but building a nine-justice majority had cost the ruling its teeth. Just a year later, the Court in Brown II walked back its commitment to equal rights and rejected calls for immediate, federally-enforced desegregation.

Before Brown II was decided, South Carolina, Georgia, and Mississippi adopted constitutional amendments authorizing their legislatures to end public education if the Court ordered immediate desegregation.133 Other strategists developed policies disguised as desegregation plans that instead stopped desegregation in its tracks.

In March 1955, North Carolina became the first state to pass a pupil placement law.134 Marian

Wright Edelman, then a young black civil rights lawyer named Marian A. Wright, called the policy "legalistic horseplay to keep Negro children out of white schools." By authorizing local school districts to assign students to schools based on a long list of subjective, "race-neutral" criteria, the law maintained nearly all-white schools without explicit legal segregation. In the words of historian Earl Black, the "North Carolina Way" ended "school desegregation at a seemly pace, one approximating the crawl of an arthritic turtle."

Okay, I'm going to come up for air for just a second and air just a few grievances. First and foremost, is why did the South ever adopt this romanized version of both the Antebellum period and the Civil War to begin with? They want us that they committed outright treason against the United States in order to own other human beings, which had thriving civilizations while we as white people were still trying to discover fire in the caves of Europe.

Second, why in the world would anyone want to deny anyone a public-school education? I mean nowadays a High School diploma is about as worth about as much as the paper it is printed on. Besides, a college degree is what is necessary for most "good" jobs. But most employers are really looking for a Masters degree in some fields. Like I said in a previous paragraph, poorly skilled people ensure there will always be an underclass to make up the "servant" class.

And finally, why people, especially whites, are so damn afraid of Blacks, Hispanics and Muslims that they run, not walk, not crawl, but run to the suburbs, leaving our once beautiful cities to rot with crime, drugs and poverty. But in the suburbs, all was well, finely manicured lawns with a lovely Cape Cod house and a high achieving school within walking distance. And all was well, right? The answer will be discussed in the next chapter.

In May 1955, the Court issued Brown II, in which it ordered schools to integrate "with all deliberate speed." The decision approved gradualism, imposed no deadlines for beginning or completing integration, issued vague guidelines, and granted Southern district judges broad discretionary oversight. Hailed as a "very definite victory for the South," the ruling pleased many pro-segregation legal and political strategists and emboldened states to undermine courts' desegregation orders.

Louisiana voters overwhelmingly approved a constitutional amendment that allowed the state to use its police powers to keep schools segregated.140 In Virginia, Prince Edward County officials stopped funding public education,141 and North Carolina devised a plan that permitted local communities to close public schools by popular vote if they were threatened with imminent desegregation.142

North Carolina's pupil placement law survived legal challenge in 1957, and by 1958, every other Southern state had passed their own.143 Alabama legislators explicitly declared that the state's placement plan was intended to block integration, but in 1958, a unanimous Supreme Court nonetheless upheld the law. Alabama officials were "jubilant," and Senator Russell Long of Louisiana said the decision was "the most encouraging thing for the South in some time," as it "shows a willingness of the court to settle for token integration."

Indeed, though Brown ruled that segregated schools harmed black students and violated their rights as Americans, Brown II prioritized the rights and preferences of white parents by enabling delay. State legislatures passed bills to thwart desegregation through "freedom-of-choice plans, which allowed parents to choose among several schools; transfer options, which permitted parents to move their children out of integrated schools; and grade-a-year plans, which started desegregation in the first or twelfth grade and then expanded it to one additional grade every year."

Pro-segregation lawmakers vocally opposed Brown. In March 1956, most of the South's representatives in Congress — 19 senators and 77 representatives — signed Virginia senator

Harry Byrd's Southern Manifesto on Integration, which condemned Brown as a "clear abuse of judicial power" orchestrated by "outside agitators" and pledged the South to all "lawful means" of resistance.

Strom Thurmond, former South Carolina Governor and Dixiecrat presidential candidate, was elected to the Senate in 1954 and helped draft the document. The legislatures of eight Southern states; Alabama, Arkansas, Florida, Georgia, Louisiana, Mississippi, South Carolina, and Virginia, also enacted "interposition" resolutions that denounced Brown as an "illegal encroachment" on state's rights and declared it "null, void and of no effect."

Virtually no desegregation occurred in any states of the former Confederacy until 1957, leading one black congressman to concede that the South had won "the first round in the battle for compliance" with Brown. One exception was Clinton, Tennessee, where the integration of a small-town high school in 1956 led to prolonged violence by enraged white mobs organized by White Citizens' Councils.

After Brown, a federal judge ordered the local high school in Clinton, Tennessee, to integrate by the start of the 1956-57 school year, and a small group of black students dubbed the "Clinton Twelve" registered to attend class with 800 white students. John Kasper of the Seaboard White Citizens' Council quickly arrived in Clinton, where he urged white students to boycott classes and community members to protest integration. A few days after students began classes, the crowd of pro-segregation protestors had grown to between 500 and 1000 people and the local sheriff sent the black student's home "for their own safety."

That evening, Kasper led 800 people in an anti-integration rally on the lawn of the Anderson County courthouse. The next day, more than 200 white students boycotted class and the mob outside the school grew increasingly violent, assaulting a black woman as she passed on the street and breaking a window at the local police station. "We need all the rabble rousers we can get," Kasper told a crowd of white supporters in Birmingham a few weeks later. "We want trouble and we want it everywhere we can get it. a collapse of law and order is near at hand."

Kasper was jailed for contempt of court, and Asa Carter of the North Alabama White Citizens' Council took over leadership of the Clinton opposition. Clinton had just 4000 residents, but Carter rallied a mob of more than 1000 people for several nights, giving speeches attacking the Supreme Court and the NAACP as agents of "mongrelization" through "race mixing." His enraged audience assaulted black motorists and pedestrians, burned a cross on the Clinton High School lawn, and faced off with local police until, at the mayor's request, the governor sent in the state highway patrol and national guard.

White violence escalated even after troops arrived. Segregationists shot into a home occupied by the father of one of the Clinton Twelve, threw dynamite into the black community of a nearby town, and attempted to lynch two black men held in the local jail. Seventy miles away, a mob of five white men confronted two white national guardsmen near the town of Dayton and asked if they would go to Clinton to enforce integration if ordered; when one of the guardsmen answered that he would, one of the men attacked him with a knife.

School resumed in Clinton after Labor Day. Troops departed and white student attendance gradually increased, but tensions remained.159 On September 26, 1956, dynamite exploded in a field next to the home of one of the Clinton Twelve. 160 On December 4, a white minister who escorted the black students to classes was beaten by enraged whites as he returned home. 161 On February 14, the black section of Clinton suffered at least eight dynamite explosions and, a week later, only seven of the original Clinton Twelve remained at Clinton High School, where they experienced attacks and harassment throughout the year.162 On October 5, 1958, two years after black students first integrated Clinton High School, the school was heavily damaged in a pre-dawn bombing.163

In the fall of 1957, 11 black students entered schools in three North Carolina cities and 11 entered white schools in Nashville, where an elementary school was destroyed by a dynamite explosion one day after it held integrated classes.

Nine black students attempting to enroll at all-white Little Rock Central High School that September were confronted by angry white crowds of students and adults and blocked by Arkansas National Guard troops commanded by Governor Orval Faubus. When President Dwight Eisenhower sent federal troops to escort the Little Rock Nine into school, hundreds of white people attacked black residents and reporters, causing nationally publicized "chaos, bedlam, and turmoil" that led a federal court to halt desegregation. The Supreme Court overturned that decision and ordered immediate integration, but in a move voters later approved in a referendum, Faubus closed all public high schools in Little Rock for the 1958-1959 school year.

No Southern state made any further progress toward desegregation until 1959, when Virginia admitted 21 black students to seven previously white schools in two cities, and two formerly all-white schools in Miami, Florida, gained black students.

By 1960, only 98 of Arkansas's 104,000 black students attended desegregated schools; as did 34 of 302,000 in North Carolina; 169 of 146,000 in Tennessee; and 103 of 203,000 in Virginia. In the five Deep South states, every single one of 1.4 million black schoolchildren attended segregated schools until the fall of 1960.166

By the start of the 1964-65 school year, less than 3 percent of the South's African American children attended school with white students, and in Alabama, Arkansas, Georgia, Mississippi, and South Carolina that number remained substantially below 1 percent.

After Brown, a federal judge ordered the local high school in Clinton, Tennessee, to integrate by the start of the 1956-57 school year, and a small group of black students dubbed the "Clinton Twelve" registered to attend class with 800 white students.150 John Kasper of the Seaboard White Citizens' Council quickly arrived in Clinton, where he urged white students to boycott classes and community members to protest integration.151 A few days after students began classes, the crowd of pro-segregation protestors had grown to between 500 and 1000 people and the local sheriff sent the black students home "for their own safety."

That evening, Kasper led 800 people in an anti-integration rally on the lawn of the Anderson County courthouse. The next day, more than 200 white students boycotted class and the mob outside the school grew increasingly violent, assaulting a black woman as she passed on the street and breaking a window at the local police station. "We need all the rabble rousers we can get," Kasper told a crowd of white supporters in Birmingham a few weeks later. "We want trouble and we want it everywhere we can get it — a collapse of law and order is near at hand."

Kasper was jailed for contempt of court, and Asa Carter of the North Alabama White Citizens' Council took over leadership of the Clinton opposition. Clinton had just 4000 residents, but Carter rallied a mob of more than 1000 people for several nights, giving speeches attacking the Supreme Court and the NAACP as agents of "mongrelization" through "race mixing." His enraged audience assaulted black motorists and pedestrians, burned a cross on the Clinton High School lawn, and faced off with local police until, at the mayor's request, the governor sent in the state highway patrol and national guard.

White violence escalated even after troops arrived. Segregationists shot into a home occupied by the father of one of the Clinton Twelve, threw dynamite into the black community of a nearby town, and attempted to lynch two black men held in the local jail. Seventy miles away, a mob of five white men confronted two white national guardsmen near the town of Dayton and asked if they would go to Clinton to enforce integration if ordered; when one of the guardsmen answered that he would, one of the men attacked him with a knife.

School resumed in Clinton after Labor Day. Troops departed and white student attendance gradually increased, but tensions remained. On September 26, 1956, dynamite exploded in a field next to the home of one of the Clinton Twelve. On December 4, a white minister who escorted the black students to classes was beaten by enraged whites as he returned home. On February 14, the black section of Clinton suffered at least eight dynamite explosions and, a week later, only seven of the original Clinton Twelve remained at Clinton High School, where they experienced attacks and harassment throughout the year. On October 5, 1958, two years after black students first integrated Clinton High School, the school was heavily damaged in a pre-dawn bombing.

Am I the only one around here that is slightly offended or even angered by the aforementioned paragraphs? Am I the only one angered at the behaviors that these "men" used in an attempt to keep children, mere children from getting an education, regardless of their skin color? Both while researching this book, and writing this book, both my value system and mind has been challenged throughout this experience. You see, while my parents raised me to have respect for everyone, especially women and the elderly, I have encountered many, many minorities in my travels. When I was in college, I had a very good friend named Dora, and as she put it, we were "tight." And yes, she was black and she and I had a lot of conversations regarding race. She invited me during the summer to her neighborhood barbeque. Now, mind you, I was the only Caucasian there, but after about 10 minutes talking with the people there, they asked me where I was from. I revealed I was a Hillbilly. One fellow there said that I sure knew how to eat. And I was respectful to everyone there. The "Yes Ma'am's and Yes Sir's really gained me a lot of respect from them. And they were the nicest people I had met in the city of Lexington, Kentucky. I had a standing invitation to come back anytime. The lesson I learned was that if you wanted respect you have to give respect, a lesson I carry with me to this very day and have since passed onto my children and grandson.

In the fall of 1957, 11 black students entered schools in three North Carolina cities and 11 entered white schools in Nashville, where an elementary school was destroyed by a dynamite explosion one day after it held integrated classes.

Nine black students attempting to enroll at all-white Little Rock Central High School that September were confronted by angry white crowds of students and adults and blocked by Arkansas National Guard troops commanded by Governor Orval Faubus. When President Dwight Eisenhower sent federal troops to escort the

Little Rock Nine into school, hundreds of white people attacked black residents and reporters, causing nationally publicized "chaos, bedlam, and turmoil" that led a federal court to halt desegregation. The Supreme Court overturned that decision and ordered immediate integration, but in a move, voters later approved in a referendum, Faubus closed all public high schools in Little Rock for the 1958-1959 school year.

No Southern state made any further progress toward desegregation until 1959, when Virginia admitted 21 black students to seven previously white schools in two cities, and two formerly all-white schools in Miami, Florida, gained black students. By 1960, only 98 of Arkansas's 104,000 black students attended desegregated schools; as did 34 of 302,000 in North Carolina; 169 of 146,000 in Tennessee; and 103 of 203,000 in Virginia. In the five Deep South states, every single one of 1.4 million black schoolchildren attended segregated schools until the fall of 1960.

By the start of the 1964-65 school year, less than 3 percent of the South's African American children attended school with white students, and in Alabama, Arkansas, Georgia, Mississippi, and South Carolina that number remained substantially below 1 percent.

When 11 black students integrated the white high school in the southern Delaware town of

Milford in fall 1954, the local school board
president predicted it would "blow the town
apart." Plans for a school dance triggered a mass
meeting attended by some 1500 white residents,
and after 800 people signed a petition opposing
an integrated dance, school officials canceled the
event. The black students were told to stay home
for several days, and when they returned to
school, police had to escort them through mobs
shouting, "The Bible gives authority for
segregation!" and "We just don't want our
children to go to school with Negroes!" Milford
expelled the black students and the NAACP
sued, sparking more cross burnings, rallies, and
pro-segregation demonstrations. The next year,
the Delaware Supreme Court ruled that Milford
could delay integration while awaiting guidance
from the United States Supreme Court.
Segregation persisted in Milford for 15 years,
until the last segregated school closed in 1970.

The fundamental question still remains to be
answered, "Why all the fear and mistrust?" Do
they think that Blacks are lower than them? Are
they less intelligent (Tell that to Neil Degrass
Tyson or Michael Eric Dyson?) Both men who, in
my opinion, are downright geniuses. Dr. Tyson
is an Astrophysicist, television host as well as an
author and the Dr. Tyson is a lawyer, professor,
and accomplished author. But there are still
some members of our society that would look at
both these accomplished men and all they would
see is the color of their skin.

Chapter Nine

The dramatically resurgent segregation of our public schools, now at its highest level since the death of Dr. Martin Luther King Jr. in 1968, is the dirty little secret of urban education that President Obama has not dared to challenge in forthright and compelling terms. Where the pattern cannot be reversed within the borders of an urban district, regional solutions need to be pursued.

The White House should lead this effort by creating an irresistibly enticing package of incentives to encourage wealthy suburban schools to admit inner-city children whose parents elect to send them there. These incentives might include additional per-pupil funding for each transfer student, construction funds to make more space available, funds to recruit and employ on-site advocates and mentors to ensure the social comfort and the pedagogic progress of these students, and funds to underwrite their transportation by the same convenient means that wealthy people use to transport their children to private schools—not by circuitous and exhausting bus routes, but rather by point-to-point travel, typically in small vans, from one specific urban neighborhood to one specific school or district. Most essential, a federal stipulation should require that those urban students in the greatest need (those with

lower achievement scores and those attending
the most troubled and most crowded schools)
receive priority.

In Boston, more than 30 suburbs participate in
a program similar to this, although without
federal help. One-third of all black and Hispanic
students in the city's deeply segregated system
are on the waiting list to get into this program to
attend the same successful schools that doctors'
kids and lawyers' kids traditionally enjoy. Ninety
percent or more of those who cross these lines of
class and race graduate from high school, and
almost all of them go on to higher education.

Do minority parents still believe in integration?
In the face of the bombastic rhetoric we
sometimes hear from self-appointed separatists,
almost every poll that has been taken indicates
that the vast majority of black and Hispanic
parents are convinced their children will receive
a better education in integrated classrooms.
They also agree with Dr. King and with the
judgment of the Warren Court in Brown v. Board
of Education of Topeka that separate schools
will always be inherently unequal.

People who devote their lives to tinkering with
clever ways to close the race gap by "demanding
more" of children and their principals and
teachers within segregated settings are,
knowingly or not, upholding the same failed and
tainted promises given to people in the United
States more than a century ago by Plessy v.

Ferguson. They are ripping to shreds the legacy of Brown and Dr. King. Only those oblivious to history would dare deceive us in this shameful manner.

What, then, should be done?

In the short run, we must bring vast pressure to bear on the U.S. president to implement a system of incentives like the one that I've described, or any other strategy he may contrive, to give the children of the inner-city poor the same full opportunity for first-rate integrated schooling that he himself enjoyed and is now providing his own children.

Charter schools, favored by the White House, are even more profoundly segregated than most other public schools. Magnet schools, with a few exceptions, have failed for more than 40 years to achieve more than a pittance of diversity. Principals especially should rise above the token gestures of the past and speak out on this issue with the nobility and the transcendent passion that dignify the crucial role they fill in our society.

In the longer run, we need to battle zoning laws, racial steering, and the other practices that perpetuate residential segregation and consign the black and brown and poor to isolated neighborhoods in which they are intention ally sequestered so that they cannot contaminate the lives and education of the privileged. This, however, is a goal that may take another century to meet. The short-term measures that are proposed could take effect within a year.

This is the whole crux of the segregation question. Isolating Blacks and Hispanics to less desirable neighborhoods while whites got the freedom to utilize upward mobility, not only economically, but socially to enjoy those benefits that they can pass along to their children. But again, the question begs to be asked, "Why do white children need to be insulated from minorities?" I mean have you listened to the music and seen some of the videos of the music that teens are listening to today? I'll give you a hint, Beyonce and Jason Derulo aren't white, as were some of the recording artists of the 1950's and early 1960's.

It would take tremendous courage in the president to lead the charge. But, if he wants to earn more than a racially symbolic place in history, this is his chance to do it.

When African American parents pressed for an end to legalized school segregation in the years leading up to the 1954 Brown v. Board of Education of Topeka decision, it was not the companionship of white children they were seeking for their children: It was access to educational resources. The schools white children attended had better facilities, better equipment and supplies, more curricular options, and often (although not always) more highly trained teachers than those serving black children. Black parents believed that equal access to those publicly funded resources was their children's birthright. Attending the same schools that white children did seemed the most likely means to achieve it.

Yet after years of progress toward school desegregation, largely achieved through busing and other court-ordered remedies, the combination of white flight from urban public-school districts and a series of Supreme Court decisions limiting the use of desegregation strategies have resulted in a widespread pattern of resegregation.

Because of segregated housing patterns, neighborhood schools are most often segregated schools. Not much can be done about that without housing policy that encourages the development of racially integrated neighborhoods. But that does not mean that schools serving children of color cannot be the beacons of educational opportunity for which previous generations struggled. The presence of white children should not be required to ensure students have adequate facilities, a challenging curriculum, well-qualified teachers, and a learning atmosphere conducive to success.

There are examples, past and present, of schools where children of color, regardless of family income, have achieved at high levels. The key to that success is in the constant drumbeat of high expectations conveyed by teachers and administrators working in partnership with engaged parents. Three key messages are at the heart of school success: This is important, you can do it, and we will not give up on you. These messages, are especially important for children from groups who too often have received, directly or indirectly, the messages, "You can't do it" and "We have already given up on you."

In an ideal multiracial society, the important skill of learning to interact with others different from oneself would be achieved along with learning to read, write, and reason quantitatively. But racially mixed environments do not guarantee that skill. Unless the learning environment is one where all children are expected to perform at a high level, the lesson that white children and children of color learn is too often a reinforcement of racial hierarchies and ideology about assumed inferiority and superiority. We cannot afford to keep teaching that old lesson. We must invest in the potential of all our children if we are to compete globally. That means investing in high-quality education no matter who is sitting in the classroom.

Educators in segregated, high-poverty school districts don't usually have time to reflect on the causes and consequences of growing racial and economic isolation. Their concerns are immediate and often urgent: maintaining adequate budgets, retaining teachers, nudging up test scores. Urging "desegregation" might seem futile in places where 90 percent of students are African American or Latino and where government-enforced boundary lines determine the demographics of schools. But segregation is not immutable. And it is harmful.

Segregation is not only harmful, but detrimental to everyone.

Concerned educators can begin by contributing their insights and public support to the National Coalition on School Diversity (NCSD), a network of national civil rights organizations and others (my own organization is a member) advocating a greater commitment to racial and economic diversity in federal policy and funding. NCSD urges federal government officials to increase funding for voluntary, public magnet schools that enroll a diverse student body. We ask that the government issue official guidance on how local school boards can legally achieve racial diversity. We advocate for funding to allow students in segregated metropolitan areas to cross district lines to attend school. At other levels of government, educators can advocate for fair and affordable housing in suburban communities and for creation of regional magnet schools that enroll students from a variety of municipalities.

As we work to change laws, regulations, and funding, we must also strive to counteract the negative effects of segregation. Segregation is not merely physical apartness. It cuts students off from the so-called "mainstream" society they must learn to navigate. Therefore, we must deliberately connect students to the society beyond their schools. Vague, rhetorical quests for "excellence" and unrelenting drilling for standardized tests will not prepare young people for full membership in society. Providing children in high-poverty segregated schools with opportunities middle-class kids take for granted will begin to close the gap. A caring school culture is vital. So are healthy food, music lessons, art programs, safe recreational space, travel opportunities, and access to mental health counseling—as well as any experience providing first-hand knowledge of life and expectations at colleges and universities and in professional settings. These opportunities are all necessary and, sadly, are not present in the lives of hundreds of kids I've known whose zip codes force them to attend schools that cannot provide adequate training for life, learning, and work.

Segregation of low-income and ethnic minority students makes closing achievement gaps virtually impossible. Separate is not equal, and never has been. In addition, this segregation is harmful to all children who will need the skills and experiences to live and work in a multicultural nation.

Two factors are driving school resegregation today. One is a political climate that has fostered acceptance of school segregation. The populace has been made to believe that there is something un-American about reassigning students to schools for the purposes of integrating education. Yet hundreds of thousands of students board school buses daily to arrive at the school of their choice.

The second factor is housing policies that support segregated neighborhoods. Increasing immigration and rising housing costs have created concentrations of single ethnic groups in inner cities where they can find affordable housing. Placing low-income and subsidized housing in integrated and suburban areas would create natural desegregation of schools, but such policies have hardly been pursued in the United States in the last several decades. We have far less subsidized housing than most modern nations, and what we do provide suffers from the NIMBY—"not in my backyard"—syndrome.

Districts must also create more magnet and dual-immersion schools in which students receive instruction in two languages. Dual-immersion schools naturally desegregate students, and middle-class parents wait in line overnight to get their children into strong programs that will enable their children to become multilingual. Mayors and educators also need to talk about how to place attractive new schools in gentrifying inner cities where the new middle class can send its children. It would be good for cities, good for business, and good for the social fabric of the nation.

To change the situation over the long run, we must (1) increase subsidized housing; (2) locate it in places that will give children access to strong integrated schools; and (3) reassign students to schools that will integrate them racially, socioeconomically, and linguistically. These recommendations will no doubt require legislative action, but educators should also organize around these issues. It's time to stand up and be counted on integration—something that is absolutely crucial to the future of public education.

Whether or not you want to admit it, our country is getting browner, thanks in part to an increase in the Hispanic population, which was here long before America was even founded! So how can you call someone an invader when they have already been here for generations? What two things disturbs me the most about the current President is first off during his 2016 campaign, he stated in several of his rallies that Mexico was sending murderers, rapists and drugs into this country, oh and "a few good people." Clearly, Candidate Trump had mastered the art of dog whistling, and no one stood up to him and corrected him. When he became President, he continued with the same strategy, and his supporters ate it up. While the rest of us started taking notice and pointing it out to everyone. Naturally we were called "snowflakes" and "Libtards," because we didn't recognize Trump as the God king that he was. Even with a

100-year pandemic raging all over the world, Trump continued with the dog whistling, calling it, "The Chinese Virus," and told Americans all would be fine in just a couple of weeks. Well, four months in and 180K deaths and nothing could be further from the truth.

The second issue I have is with the current Secretary of Education, Betsy DeVos. Now, Ms. DeVos is an interesting person. She has never spent one day as either a student or as a parent of a public school. Nor has she attended a public college or university. What made her qualified? A rather large campaign contribution to Trump's Presidential campaign. Oh, and did I mention she is a big fan of charter schools, which syphons money set aside for public schools and is generally a for profit venture. And since they are considered a "private" school, they are exempt from the "separation of church and state" rulings set forth by Supreme Court rulings, in other words, a conservative's wet dreams. Now, of course the Trump supporters are behind this idea 100% because it keeps "those people" out of little Johnnie's or Jill's school. But I see something more sinister afoot. You see, those education dollars syphoned off are not earmarked for any one particular type of school or school district, they are earmarked for ALL schools and if it is all earmarked for charter schools, none will be available, and the public schools will have to shutter their doors. And what would happen to all those children now left without an education? Simple, the Child Labor laws would have to be abolished, allowing for an entirely new group of labor to be exploited. Again, something for the conservatives to go off foaming at the mouth.

Chapter Ten

As promised, this chapter is going to briefly to discuss the School to Prison pipeline, or SPP. This is where the schools have developed zero tolerance policies for student behaviors and in effect criminalized those behaviors enough to require law enforcement intervention. This policy covers everything from truancy to fighting to acting out behaviors in elementary school children. Did I mention that these policies unfairly target both Black and Hispanic children? Well, it does.

Usually every school district has a School Resource Officer (SRO,) these initially were put in place in the schools immediately following the school shootings at Columbine High School in Littleton, Colorado with the singular purpose of preventing school shootings, However, over the past twenty years their roles have greatly expanded. Did they stop school shootings? Not really. Lakeland, Florida proved that wrong

I fondly remember my time as a school social worker and the students I helped. I also had a very close working relationship with the School Resource Officer, but we usually were looking for illegal drugs. I personally even once prevented a possible school shooting, after a "hit list" was found by a student, who by the way later called me to confess that it was she who had written this list. But I digress. The other social worker and I would listen to the other students talk, and they would slip up and mention where their dealer or they had hidden their stash and one or both of up would go to his office, tell him what we had heard and go hunting for the drugs. Nine times out of ten, we found it. I was even asked to identify some drugs students were trying to sell. Once, I was handed a baggie of pills and was asked if I knew what they were? I recognized them immediately and told them they were Adderall 10's, which were usually prescribed for AD/HD, but in late teens and adults, it is a powerful stimulant.

The current sociopolitical climate, relating to mass incarceration in the United States and calls for decarceration, serves as a critical component in increasing the contact the incarceration system has with the United States education system, as patterns of criminalization translate into the school context. Specific practices implemented in United States schools over the past ten years to reduce violence in schools, including zero tolerance policies and an increase in School Resource Officers have created the environment for criminalization of youth in schools. This results from patterns of discipline in schools mirroring law enforcement models.

The disciplinary policies and practices that create an environment for the United States school-to-prison link to occur disproportionately affect disabled, Latino and Black students which is later reflected in the rates of incarceration. Between 1999 and 2007, the percentage of black students being suspended has increased by twelve percent, while the percentage of white students being suspended has declined since the implementation of zero tolerance policies. Of the total incarcerated population in the United States, 61% are Black or Latino.

Zero tolerance policies are school disciplinary policies that set predetermined consequences or punishments for specific offenses. By nature. zero tolerance policies, as any policy that is "unreasonable rule or policy that is the same for everyone but has an unfair effect on people who share a particular attribute" often become discriminatory. The zero tolerance approach was first introduced in the 1980s to reduce drug use in schools. The use of zero tolerance policies spread more widely in the 1990s. To reduce gun violence, the Gun Free Schools Act of 1994 (GFSA) required that schools receiving federal funding "must 1) have policies to expel for a calendar year any student who brings a firearm to school or to school zone, and 2) report that student to local law enforcement, thereby blurring any distinction between disciplinary infractions at school and the law."[1] During the 1996-1997 school year, 94% of schools had zero tolerance policies for fire arms, 87% for alcohol, and 79% for violence. So much for the students in Eastern Kentucky and in West Virginia having their deer rifles on school property so they could go hunting immediately after school.

Over the past decade, zero tolerance policies have expanded to predetermined punishments for a wide degree of rule violations. Zero-tolerance policies do not distinguish between serious and non-serious offenses. All students who commit a given offense receive the same treatment. Behaviors punished by zero tolerance policies are most often non-serious offense and are punished on the same terms as a student would be for bringing a gun or drugs to school. In 2006, 95% of out-of-school suspensions were for nonviolent, minor disruptions such as tardiness. In 2006-2007, "out-of-school suspensions for non-serious, non-violent offenses accounted for 37.2% of suspensions in Maryland, whereas only 6.7% of suspensions were issued for dangerous behaviors." In Chicago, the widespread adoption of zero-tolerance policies in 1994 resulted in a 51% increase in student suspensions for the next four years and a 3,000% increase in expulsions. All the zero-tolerance policy did was elevate age appropriate acting out behaviors to the levels which require suspension or expulsion. This would be a situation better suited for a school social worker or a school-based therapist, not disciplinary or by law enforcement intervention.

The most direct way these policies increase the probability of a youth coming into contact with the incarceration system is through their exclusionary methods. Suspension, expulsion, and an increased risk of dropping out all contribute to a youth's increased chances of becoming involved with the incarceration system. Suspension removes students from the structure and supervision provided through schooling, providing opportunities for youth to engage in criminal activities while not in the school environment. Other factors may include "increased exposure to peers involved in antisocial behavior, as well as effects on school performance and completion and student attitudes toward antisocial behavior." Suspension can lead to feelings of alienation from the school setting that can lead to students to feel rejected, increasing chances of relationships with antisocial peers. Relationships with peers have strong impacts on student behavior, demonstrated through differential association theory. Students are more than twice as likely to be arrested during months in which they are forcibly removed from school. Students who have been suspended are three times more likely to drop out by the 10th grade than students who have never been suspended. Dropping out makes that student three times more likely to be incarcerated. There is nothing achievable when a student drops out, In fact, I was responsible for a "drop-in" program where students who dropped out came back to school, made a little money in doing so, and earned their diploma. I had a 50% success rate in year one. When the students heard that I might not be returning the next school year, they "Christmas treed" the exit exam. I had to tell them that I did not make the program a success or failure, they did. This time they retook the exam correctly.

Zero tolerance policies increase the number of School Resource Officers (SRO) in schools, which increases the contact a student has with the criminal justice system. Students may be referred by teachers or other administrators but most often zero tolerance policies are directly enforced by police or school resource officers. The practice of increasing the number of police in schools contributes to patterns of criminalization. This increase in SROs has led to contemporary school discipline beginning to mirror approaches used in legal and law enforcement. Zero tolerance policies increase the use of profiling, a very common practice used in law enforcement. This practice is able to identify students who may engage in misbehavior, but the use of profiling is unreliable in ensuring school safety, as this practice over identifies students from minority populations. There were no students involved in the 1990s shootings who were Black or Latino and the 1990s school shootings were the main basis for the increase in presence of police in schools. If I am not mistaken, there has been NO Black or Latino school shooters, all have been white, middle class students.

A Justice Policy Institute report (2011) found a 38% increase in the number of SROs between 1997 and 2007 as a result of the growing implementation of zero tolerance policies.[9] In 1999, 54% of students surveyed reported seeing a security guard or police officer in their school, by 2005, this number increased to 68%. The education system has seen a huge increase in the number of students referred to law enforcement. In one city in Georgia, when police officers were introduced into the schools, "school-based referrals to juvenile court in the county increased 600% over a three-year period." There was no increase in the number of serious offenses or safety violations during this three-year period.[35] In 2012, forty-one states required schools to report students to law enforcement for various misbehaviors on school grounds. This practice increases the use of law enforcement professionals in handling student behavior and decreases the use of in-classroom (non-exclusionary) management of behaviors.

In 2014, the United Nations Human Rights Committee (HRC) expressed concern with increasing criminalization of students in response to school disciplinary problems, and recommended that the US government "promote the use of alternatives to the application of criminal law" to address such issues. The HRC also noted its concern with the use of corporal punishment in schools in the US. In the second Universal Periodic Review of the United States' human-rights record, the government avowed taking "effective measures to help ensure non-discrimination in school discipline policies and practices."

One of the major drivers of this is the current editorial stance in America today. A substantial body of research claims that incarceration rates are primarily a function of media editorial policies, largely unrelated to the actual crime rate. Beginning especially in the 1970s, the mainstream commercial media in the U.S. increased coverage of the police blotter, while reducing coverage of investigative journalism. This had at least two advantages for the commercial media organizations:

Poor people can be libeled and slandered with impunity, and stories based on interviewing police are easy and cheap to create.

This reduces the space that might otherwise be filled with investigative journalism, which too often threatens major advertisers.

Advertising rates are set based on the audience. Because "if it bleeds, it leads," the media were able to accomplish this change without losing audience.

Beyond this, the growth of private prisons increased the pool of major advertisers who could be offended by honest reporting on incarcerations and the school-to-prison pipeline: It makes financial sense to report on this only to the extent that such reporting is needed to maintain an audience.

There you have just a small sample of what Black and Hispanic students have to face besides being marginalized once again by this move to resegregate school systems. As white parents, fearful of what their precious little ones will be exposed to should any of "those people" be allowed to attend the same school as their children, shouldn't have such fears. They act as if suburbia is the last fortress for whiteness in America.

 Will I be examining this in the future? YES! Will I Be writing a book on this topic sometime in the future? YES!

Chapter Eleven

America's schools are more racially segregated than they've been in decades. Between 2001 and 2014, the number of schools that are more 90 percent low-income students of color more than doubled. Half a century after Jim Crow officially ended, more than one in five students attended racially segregated schools last year in Alabama, Louisiana, and Mississippi, according to a recent report from Loyola University in New Orleans. A 2014 study from the University of California-Los Angeles found that schools in the South are as segregated as they were in 1967.

Since 2000, hundreds of schools have been released from federal desegregation orders, and this has led many Southern communities to redraw attendance boundaries in ways that result in schools that are more racially and economically segregated. After the Tuscaloosa City Schools in Alabama were released from a court order, for example, the city's large, integrated high school was replaced by three smaller schools — one of which is 99 percent black.

Some school districts that were intentionally segregated after the U.S. Supreme Court's 1954 Brown v. Board of Education decision against segregated schools are still under court desegregation orders dating back decades. Most of them are in the Deep South.

Civil rights advocates are concerned that the Trump administration is embracing policies that will drive resegregation. For instance, the Justice Department backed the request of a Mississippi school system seeking to be released from its desegregation order — a reversal from the Department's position before Trump took office. And Trump Education Secretary Betsy DeVos eliminated her department's Opening Doors program, which aimed to encourage voluntary desegregation. DeVos is also a prominent backer of school vouchers and charter schools, which are contributing to resegregation in many states.

The Trump administration has been for almost four years, covert about their contempt for Blacks. Now they are blatantly overt in their contempt of Hispanics. So, it stands to reason that this administration would like to see nothing better than all little white children is all white schools and all other minorities elsewhere, out of sight, of mind. Never in my life have I've seen an administration so determined to reinstitute the concept of separate, yet unequal. Secretary DeVos is just a prime example of someone who wants to institutionalize resegregation as a matter of public policy.

In Brown, the U.S. Supreme Court ruled that segregated schools are unconstitutional. "In the field of public education, the doctrine of 'separate but equal' has no place," the ruling said. "Separate educational facilities are inherently unequal." The Supreme Court and the U.S. Department of Justice, empowered to sue school districts under the Civil Rights Act of 1964, pushed recalcitrant Southern school systems to integrate in the 1960s and 1970s.

School integration hit its peak in the late 1980s, when more than 40 percent of black students attended majority-white schools. Since then, a more conservative Supreme Court has chipped away at this progress. The Court has "actively thwarted public-school desegregation even in districts where democratically elected leaders support increased efforts at integration," noted Ian Millhiser of ThinkProgress.

In 2007, the Court ruled that voluntary integration efforts in Seattle and Louisville, Kentucky, were unconstitutional. The opinion by Chief Justice John Roberts compared the voluntary integration plans to Jim Crow schools, though acknowledging they were enacted "for very different reasons."

This is due to the conservative leanings of the Supreme Court, which views America in a "post-racial" lens. The conscrvative's belief the we "elected a Black President," so we are all good, right? Is so far off the mark it is not even funny. They fail to recognize 400 years of slavery, 150 years of Jim Crow laws, as well as countless acts of discrimination, including redlining, which made it nearly impossible for blacks to get a home loan, never allowing them to fully participate in the American Dream,

Communities across the South, however, have begun dividing up school districts — splitting more integrated countywide systems into wealthier suburban and poorer urban districts. Some legislatures have gotten involved in those efforts. In 2015, for instance, Florida lawmakers introduced a bill to allow school district secession, though it did not pass. And in North Carolina, the General Assembly recently considered allowing communities to incorporate their own school systems. North Carolina's largest districts, which include the cities of Charlotte and Raleigh, were once models of desegregation, but a recent report from the N.C. Justice Center found intensifying resegregation across the state in the last decade.

Many court desegregation orders require judicial approval before districts can be split up. For example, federal courts have allowed several districts to secede from Alabama's Jefferson County school district, which includes the city of Birmingham. But in February, the 11th U.S. Circuit Court of Appeals rejected a request by the Birmingham suburb of Gardendale to secede from Jefferson County. The trial court found that Gardendale activists and local legislators pushing to secede had "acted with a discriminatory purpose to exclude black children from the proposed system."

The 11th Circuit agreed, noting that the "Gardendale secession movement started when the schools in that City were becoming racially diverse," thanks to a desegregation order that allowed students to transfer between county schools. In an opinion by Judge William Pryor, a Republican appointee, the 11th Circuit found that secession would also thwart desegregation efforts and send "messages of inferiority" to the black students. The court rejected concerns about how students and parents might react to its ruling, noting that the desegregation that followed Brown wouldn't have happened "if animosity alone could thwart constitutional imperatives."

A Trump judicial nominee, Tennessee state Sen. Mark Norris, has come under fire for his personal role in the resegregation of schools in the Memphis area. After a federal court ordered desegregation by busing in 1973, white families fled the Memphis district for other communities in Shelby County. By 2010, 86 percent of the municipal district's student body was black, while white students were a majority in the county. That year, the city district voluntary surrendered its charter and allowed the district to be absorbed by the county.

Norris responded by authoring a bill to create an exception to the state's ban on cities and town incorporating their own school districts that would apply only to Shelby County. The bill delayed the merger for three years and "pacified the county's largest and wealthiest suburbs by creating the legal means for their secession," according to law professor Michelle Wilde Anderson. A Democratic legislator said the goal of the bill was "to allow those four or five towns in Shelby County to be able to form their white school districts." Six communities established separate school districts, robbing the remaining county schools of much-needed resources.

Given the crucial role that federal courts continue to play in desegregation, civil rights advocates are concerned about Trump's judicial nominees, two of whom are facing criticism for refusing to state that Brown was correctly decided. Asked about the case during their confirmation hearings, Wendy Vitter and Andrew Oldham, nominated to the 5th U.S. Circuit Court of Appeals that hears cases from Texas, Louisiana, and Mississippi, declined to comment on Brown or other specific cases, even though some past Circuit Court nominees have unequivocally endorsed Brown.

Racial polarization in schools has only risen since 2000, according to the Government Accountability Office. This trend can be directly tied to residential segregation in communities surrounding educational institutions. The Federal data from 2016 shows that poor black and Hispanic children are becoming increasingly isolated from white, affluent children in America's public and private schools and as a result are limited in their exposure to basic resources, supplies and even classrooms. The rash inequalities across the lines of race and class that have been exemplified by recent events are not unfamiliar. Our country has begun to seriously regress over the last 65 years since the Brown v. Board of Education ruling officially desegregated schools.

In the civil rights era, nearly 80% of public-school students were white, and African American students were the largest group among students of color. In the last school year for which my group had data, 2016 to 2017, the U.S. public schools no longer had a majority of any racial group.

Despite an increase in the number of public-school students since the late 1960s, there are almost 11 million fewer white children in public schools nearly 50 years later. However, white students are still the largest group of students at 48%.

Latino students continue to increase nationally and in every region of the country. There are also 1 million more black students since the civil rights era, or approximately 15% of students. In some states, Asian students are increasing. Multiracial students – a group not even part of the official federal classification until 2008 – are also nearly 4%.

However, white students and students of color are unevenly distributed across schools, and these differences affect their experiences in schools and classrooms. If a school were perfectly integrated, students' exposure to students of other races would match the national racial composition of students. But white students have lower exposure to students of other races than any other group of students. The typical white student attends a school that is 69% white. This is considerably higher than white students' national share of the enrollment.

White students also have only 31% of students who are of other races, on average, in their schools. By this measure, white students are more segregated than any other group. Having limited cross-racial exposure, these students miss out on valuable benefits of such experiences. Children with more exposure to people of other races are less likely to stereotype and more likely to seek out diverse experiences as adults. However, I'm encouraged by the fact that white isolation has decreased in recent years, as the public-school enrollment has become more diverse. The average black or Latino student also goes to a school with a relatively high share of students of their own race.

Additionally, more than 40% of black and Latino students attend intensely segregated schools, where at least 9 in 10 students are people of color. Most of these schools have a majority of low-income students, which a 2016 government report concluded harmed students' educational opportunities. The percentages of black and Latino students in intensely segregated schools have risen since late 1980s, after the Reagan Justice Department stopped asking courts to implement busing as a remedy in desegregation cases.

It is also a hot button topic is the fact that the occupants of the suburbs are afraid that minorities will come in and bring all the stereotypically negative things into their neighborhood. The Republican party is preying on that fear in hopes that white suburban housewives will be afraid of the consequences of this. Yet, the Republican party continues to play this card of all the negative things regarding race in this country just to win elections when it is their policies that intentionally keeps Blacks from fully having a seat at the table. It was a Southern Senator who once said, "The problem with the Republican party is that it is no longer generating enough angry old white men." Now what a statement to make, saying that the political party's very survival is predicated upon having sufficient numbers of angry white voters. And desegregation is one of those trigger issues which will get voters ire up. And again, the question continues to be asked, "Why?"

Chapter Twelve

Do we have an answer yet as to why segregation is needed in the third decade of the twenty-first century? No? Good, me neither.

Three years before Brown v. Board in November 1951, students in a civics class at the segregated black Adkin High School in Kinston, North Carolina, discussed what features an ideal school should have for a class assignment. When they realized that the local white high school indeed had everything they had imagined, the seeds were planted for a student-led protest. Without the assistance from any adults, these students confronted the local school board about the blatant inequality of local schools. When the board ignored their request for more funding, the students met by themselves to plan what to do next. In a group interview with these former students, John Dudley remembers, "So, that week, leading to Monday, we strategized. And we had everybody on board, 720 students. We told them not to tell your parents or your teacher what's going on. And do you believe to this day, 2013, nobody has ever told me that an adult knew what was going on. Kids." They decided on a coded phrase that was read during morning announcements. Every student in the school walked out, picked up placards that had been made in advance, and marched downtown to protest. The students refused to go back to school for a week, and eighteen months later, Adkin High School was renovated and given a brand-new gymnasium. It would remain segregated until 1970, however.

Desegregation was not always a battle in every community in the South. Lawrence Guyot, who later became a leader in the Student Nonviolent Coordinating Committee, grew up in Pass Christian, a city on the Mississippi Gulf Coast that was influenced by the strong labor unions in the shipyard industry and the Catholic Church. He explains how the Catholic schools were desegregated there: "The Catholic Church in 1957 or '58 made a decision that they were going to desegregate the schools. They did it this way. The announcement was we have two programs. We have excommunication and we have integration. Make your choice by Friday. Now there was violence going on in Louisiana. Nothing happened on the Gulf Coast. I learned firsthand that institutions can really have an impact on social policy."

In an interview about his mother, civil rights activist Gayle Jenkins, Willie "Chuck" Jenkins describes how she demanded that he would be the plaintiff in a school desegregation suit, Jenkins v. Bogalusa School Board in Louisiana. He became the first African American student to attend the white Bogalusa Junior High School in 1967 and remembers how he had one foot in each world, but was increasingly alienated from both: "And I caught a lot of slack, like, from the black community, because they used to say, 'Oh, you think you're something because you're going to the white school.' They didn't know I was catching holy hell at the white school. I had no friends, you know. So, it was just always a conflict." But in the end, he thinks it was worth it. He states, "But it was hard, but you know what? If I had it to do all over again, I would do it exactly the same way. Because it was a cause that was well worth the outcome, even though I feel like people in Bogalusa are still not as accepting as they could be." The high school continued to have a separate white prom and a black prom until very recently. But his mother, Gayle Jenkins, would serve on the Bogalusa School Board for twenty-seven years.

While Brown v. Board of Education and many other legal cases broke down the official barriers for African Americans to gain an equal education, achieving this ideal has never been easy or simple. The debate continues today among policy makers, educators, and parents about how to close the achievement gap between minority and white children. Ruby Sales, a former Student Nonviolent Coordinating Committee (SNCC) member who later became the founder and director of the nonprofit organization Spirt House, points out that few people look to the past for answers to our current problems in education: "...We have been dealing with the counter-culture of education, and what might we learn from that counter-culture during segregation that would enable black students not to be victims in public schools today. And one of the things that disturbed me so tremendously, and this is about narrative again: these southern black teachers created outstanding students and leaders. And many of them still exist. And no one has bothered to ask them, "How did you do it? What might we learn from you? What were your strategies? How did you deal with complicated situations? How did you invigorate young people to believe that they could make a difference even when the white world said that they couldn't?"

But that is an age-old question, how does one as a teacher ignite the spark of learning within a student? Can we tap into their cultural and historical heritage? Do we do immersion teaching or some other form of pedagogy to engage minority students? These questions would have to be answered in a truly integrated school.

From 1968 to 1980, segregation between blacks and whites in schools declined. School integration peaked in the 1980s and then gradually declined over the course of the 1990s, as income differences increased. In the 1990s and early 2000s, minority students attended schools with a declining proportion of white students, so that the rate of segregation as measured as isolation resembled that of the 1960s. There is some disagreement about what to make of trends since the 1980s; while some researchers have presented trends as evidence of "resegregation," others argue that changing demographics in school districts, including class and income, are responsible for most of the changes in the racial composition of schools. A 2013 study by Jeremy Fiel found that, "for the most part, compositional changes are to blame for the declining presence of whites in minorities' schools," and that racial balance increased from 1993 to 2010. The study found that minority students became more isolated and less exposed to whites, but that all students became more evenly distributed across schools. Another 2013 study found that segregation measured as exposure increased over the previous 25 years due to changing demographics. The study did not, however, find an increase in racial balance; rather, racial unevenness remained stable over that time period. Researcher Kori Stroub found that the "racial/ethnic resegregation of public schools observed over the 1990s has given way to a period of modest reintegration," but that segregation between school districts has increased even though within-district segregation is low. Fiel believes that increasing interdistrict segregation will exacerbate racial isolation.

A principal source of school segregation is the persistence of residential segregation in American society; residence and school assignment are closely linked due to the widespread tradition of locally controlled schools. Residential segregation is related to growing income inequality in the United States.

A study conducted by Sean Reardon and John Yun found that from 1990 to 2000, residential black/white and Hispanic/white segregation declined by a modest amount in the United States, while public school segregation increased slightly during the same time period. Because the two variables moved in opposite directions, changes in residential patterns are not responsible for changes in school segregation trends. Rather, the study determined that in 1990, schools showed less segregation than neighborhoods, indicating that local policies were helping to ameliorate the effects of residential segregation on school composition. By 2000, however, racial composition of schools had become more closely correlated to neighborhood composition, indicating that public policies no longer redistributed students as evenly as before.

A 2013 study corroborated these findings, showing that the relationship between residential and school segregation became stronger over the decade between 2000 and 2010. In 2000, segregation of blacks in schools was lower than in their neighborhoods; by 2010, the two patterns of segregation were "nearly identical".

While greater school choice could potentially increase integration by drawing students from larger and more geographically diverse areas (as opposed to segregated neighborhoods), expanded choice often has the opposite effect. Studies conducted on the relationship between expanded school choice and school segregation show that when studies compare the racial/ethnic composition of charter schools to local public schools, researchers generally find that charter schools preserve or intensify existing racial and economic segregation, and/or facilitate white flight from public schools. Furthermore, studies that compare individual students' demographic characteristics to the schools they are leaving (public schools) and the schools they are switching to (charter schools) generally demonstrate that students "leave more diverse public schools and enroll in less diverse charter schools".

Private schools constitute a second important type of school choice. A 2002 study found that private schools continued to contribute to the persistence of school segregation in the South over the course of the 1990s. Enrollment of whites in private schools increased sharply in the 1970s, remained unchanged in the 1980s, and increased again over the course of the 1990s. Because the changes over the latter two decades was not substantial, however, researcher Sean Reardon concludes that changes in private school enrollment is not a likely contributor to any changes in school segregation patterns during that time.

In contrast to charter and private schools, magnet schools generally foster racial integration rather than hinder it. Such schools were initially presented as an alternative to unpopular busing policies, and included explicit desegregation goals along with provisions for recruiting and providing transportation for diverse populations. Although today's magnet schools are no longer as explicitly oriented towards integration efforts, they continue to be less racially isolated than other forms of school choice.

The level of racial segregation in schools has important implications for the educational outcomes of minority students. Desegregation efforts of the 1970s and 1980s led to substantial academic gains for black students; as integration increased, blacks' educational attainment increased while that of whites remained largely unchanged. Historically, greater access to schools with higher enrollments of white students helped "reduce blacks' high school dropout rate, reduce the black-white test score gap, and improve outcomes for black in areas such as earnings, health, and incarceration."

Nationwide, minority students continue to be concentrated in high-poverty, low-achieving schools, while white students are more likely to attend high-achieving, more affluent schools. Resources such as funds and high-quality teachers attach unequally to schools according to racial and socioeconomic composition. Schools with high proportions of minority enrollment are often characterized by "less experienced and less qualified teachers, high levels of teacher turnover, less successful peer groups and inadequate facilities and learning materials." These schools also tend to have less challenging curricula and fewer offerings of Advanced Placement courses.

Access to resources is not the only factor determining education outcomes; the very racial composition of schools can have an effect independent of the level of other resources. A 2009 study determined that attending school with a high proportion of black students negatively affected black academic achievement, even after controlling for school quality, differences in ability, and family background. The effect of racial composition on white achievement was insignificant.

The research that has been conducted on the effects of school segregation can be divided into studies that observe short-term and long-term outcomes of segregated schooling; these outcomes can be either academic or non-academic in nature. Studies of short-term outcomes observe the relationship between school segregation and outcomes such as academic achievement (test scores), racial prejudice/fear, and cross-cultural friendships. Long-term outcomes may refer to educational attainment, occupational attainment, adults' intergroup relations, crime and violence, and civic engagement.

The mixed findings of research on the effects of integration on black students has resulted in ambiguous conclusions as to the influence of desegregation plans. Generally, integration has a small but beneficial impact on short-term outcomes for blacks (i.e. education achievement), and a clearly beneficial impact on longer-term outcomes, such as school attainment (i.e. level of education attained) and earnings. Integrated education is positively related to short-term outcomes such as K–12 school performance, cross-racial friendships, acceptance of cultural differences, and declines in racial fears and prejudice. In the long run, integration is associated with higher educational and occupational attainment across all ethnic groups, better intergroup relations, greater likelihood of living and working in an integrated environment, lower likelihood of involvement with the criminal justice system, espousal of democratic values, and greater civic engagement.

A 1994 study found support for the theory that interracial contact in elementary or secondary school positively affects long-term outcomes in a way that can help blacks overcome perpetual segregation. The study reviewed previous research and determined that, as compared to segregated blacks, desegregated blacks are more likely to set higher occupational aspirations, attend desegregated colleges, have desegregated social and professional networks as adults, gain desegregated employment, and work in white-collar and professional jobs in the private sector.

Short-term and long-term benefits of integration are found for minority and majority students alike. Students who attend integrated schools are more likely to live in diverse neighborhoods as adults than those students who attended more segregated schools. Integrated schools also reduce the maintenance of stereotypes and prevent the formation of prejudices in both majority and minority students.

Chapter Thirteen

Desegregation didn't really get going for almost a decade after Brown, but then it finally started to take hold, reaching a peak at around 1988Opens a new window. And guess what? Integration worked. The achievement gap, for example, between white kids and Black kids closed, dramatically.

But desegregation faltered in the face of massive "white flight," when white people moved out of cities all around the US (especially in the Northeast) rather than keep their kids in integrated schools. And it ran up against the seemingly intractable legacy of racist zoning policies and racist mortgage lending that created segregated (and often impoverished) communities in our cities and suburbs.

Why did desegregation fail? Look to politics, leadership, and the courts, you'll see shifting priorities and a failure of will. And so here we are, right now, with school segregation at 1968. Separate was never equal, not decades ago and not today. This unjust and unfair system continues to put Black and Latinx children at a severe disadvantage. Indeed, the kinds of schools most white children attend may as well be located in a different world.

The problems show up as early as preschool. Remember preschool? Learning to write your name, playing with dolls and blocks, jumping in puddles. That's the preschool experience. Also part of the experience? Racism. It turns out that a disproportionate number of Black families lack access to high-quality preschool. And that when their kids do go to preschool, they're treated unfairly: Black students are much more likely to be suspended from preschool than white students.

Why is this? Does anyone really believe that Black preschoolers are simply more terribly behaved?

A 2014 study might shine some light on what's going on. Although it doesn't cover preschool-age children, it found that Black boys as young as 10 are routinely perceived to be significantly older and less innocent, when compared to white boys of the same age. In our society, this suspicion of guilt follows people of color throughout their lives.

Sadly, you won't be surprised to discover that the news doesn't get better for K-12 kids. Let's run through some of the data released by the US Department of Education in 2014:

When Black students and white students commit similar infractions, Black students are suspended and expelled three times more often than white students.

Black students make up 16% of student enrollment, but represent 27% of students referred to law enforcement and 31% of students subjected to arrest. White students, on the other hand, make up 51% of enrollment, 41% of students referred to law enforcement, and 39% of those arrested.

 The "school-to-prison pipeline" is what some have taken to calling the way school discipline increasingly involves law enforcement and channels students into the criminal justice system (where people of color can expect unfair treatment as a matter of course). When a simple altercation at school leads to an arrest for assault, something has gone terribly wrong.

Repeated suspensions and expulsions also eventually convince many students to drop out, and a huge number of those leaving school are Black, Latinx, or Native American. A 2004 study found that only about half of Black, Latinx, and Native American students graduate high school. Think about that: only half!

The racial wealth gap in America is huge, and systemic racism is responsible both for its creation and its persistence. Those zoning laws and mortgage practices we mentioned earlier have not only kept cities and communities segregated, they've ensured that people of color are unable to accumulate and pass on wealth in the way that white families can. The poverty in these communities means that schools attended predominately by people of color are chronically underfunded.

Kids who attend these schools regularly have inexperienced and even unlicensed teachers. Their academic performance suffers as a result, which can lead many to drop out, while putting the dream of college at risk for those who remain.

Our segregated education system is a mess, it's bad news all around, no doubt. What can we do? Lots of people are clearly worried about it. Education experts suggest new programs every year and write dozens of op-eds touting their supposed benefits, all while neglecting one solution that, when tried, actually worked: Desegregation. Desegregation really worked.

And beyond that, going to school with a racially diverse student body can actually reduce racism, counter stereotypes, and lead to a greater appreciation and understanding of people who are different than we are. All of which sounds like something we desperately need.

Segregation is the root cause for a lot of our social ills right now that should not even have to be in place. From redlining to police brutality to street violence all have their roots tangled in segregation. A deliberate division of haves and have-nots which our society does not need. Blacks and Hispanics have fought bravely and honorably in our armed forces, to fight for a country that won't give them respect back. It was like after World War II, when Blacks were serving over in Europe, they were treated with dignity and respect that they would never get in the United States, because the British recognized them as American GI's, not as Black men. But upon returning home, they were met with increased racism, because being overseas, white folks thought they were getting too "uppity," and forgetting their place in the social order.

Systemic racism is a corrosive and widespread problem in our society, at all levels, and we all need to do a better job of confronting it, in our neighborhoods, at our schools, and in ourselves.

White students and students of color are unevenly distributed across schools, and these differences affect their experiences in schools and classrooms. If a school were perfectly integrated, students' exposure to students of other races would match the national racial composition of students.

But white students have lower exposure to students of other races than any other group of students. The typical white student attends a school that is 69% white. This is considerably higher than white students' national share of the enrollment.

White students also have only 31% of students who are of other races, on average, in their schools. By this measure, white students are more segregated than any other group. Having limited cross-racial exposure, these students miss out on valuable benefits of such experiences. Children with more exposure to people of other races are less likely to stereotype and more likely to seek out diverse experiences as adults. However, I'm encouraged by the fact that white isolation has decreased in recent years, as the public-school enrollment has become more diverse. The average black or Latino student also goes to a school with a relatively high share of students of their own race.

Additionally, more than 40% of black and Latino students attend intensely segregated schools, where at least 9 in 10 students are people of color. Most of these schools have a majority of low-income students, which a 2016 government report concluded harmed students' educational opportunities.

The percentages of black and Latino students in intensely segregated schools have risen since late 1980s, after the Reagan Justice Department stopped asking courts to implement busing as a remedy in desegregation cases.

The South was once the most segregated region in the U.S. In the late 1960s, more than three-quarters of black students attended schools where less than 10% of students were white. This was an improvement since Brown v. Board of Education when the percentage was 100%, but the South still lagged far behind the rest of the U.S. The percentage of black students in intensely segregated schools in the South dropped dramatically until the late 1980s, down to 24%.

In fact, despite a recent rise in segregation in the South, it remains one of the least segregated regions in the U.S., leading the rest of the country in school desegregation for African American students. The opposite is true in the Northeast. Since the late 1960s, the Northeast has experienced a steady increase in the percentage of black students enrolled in schools with fewer than 10% white students. In 2016, more than half of black students were in such segregated schools.

Historically, segregation has been discussed as a southern and urban issue, relevant to places like Little Rock, Arkansas, and Boston, Massachusetts. But segregation has spread beyond central cities. In the suburbs of large metropolitan areas, white students are 47% of the enrollment. Yet, the typical black or Latino student attends a school in these suburban areas that has just over 25% white students. Even in rural areas, white students attend public schools with almost twice as many white students as do black and Latino rural students.

These trends are not inevitable. As is evident in the South, the U.S. did make considerable progress in the past. In my view, all regions of our country and rural and metropolitan areas

alike have changing patterns of segregation that
demand the public's attention and action.

Chapter Fourteen

Well over six decades after the Supreme Court declared "separate but equal" schools to be unconstitutional in Brown v. Board of Education, schools remain heavily segregated by race and ethnicity. What are the consequences of this lack of progress in integrating schools for black children?

It depresses education outcomes for black students; it lowers their standardized test scores. It widens performance gaps between white and black students. It reflects and bolsters segregation by economic status, with black students being more likely than white students to attend high-poverty schools.

It means that the promise of integration and equal opportunities for all black students remains an ideal rather than a reality. In contrast, when black students have the opportunity to attend schools with lower concentrations of poverty and larger shares of white students they perform better, on average, on standardized tests. Black children are still relegated to separate and unequal schools.

Findings on school segregation and student performance come from the National Center for Education Statistics' National Assessment of Educational Progress (NAEP), the most comprehensive study of education performance in the country. We use the most recently released data to describe school segregation and its consequences for math performance of eighth-graders. These data show that only about one in eight white students (12.9%) attends a school where a majority of students are black, Hispanic, Asian, or American Indian. We refer to this group collectively as students of color hereafter. In contrast, nearly seven in 10 black children (69.2%) attend such schools. Less than one in three white students (31.3%) attend a high-poverty school, compared with more than seven in 10 black students (72.4%). Black children are five times as likely as white children to attend schools that are highly segregated by race and ethnicity

In America, race and poverty are intertwined, doubly disadvantaging black students. The known connection between race/ethnicity and poverty in the United States appears in data on the composition of schools attended by for black children. While less than 1 in 10 white students (8.4%) attend high-poverty schools with a high share of students of color, six in 10 black students (60.0%) do.

In contrast, about a fourth of white students (23.5%) attend schools where most of their peers are white and not poor, while only 3.1 percent of black children attend such schools.

Schools with a high concentration of students of color are those in which 51– not 100% of students are black, Hispanic, Asian, or American Indian. Mostly white schools are those in which more than 75% of students are white. High-poverty schools are schools in which 51–100% of students are eligible for free or reduced-price lunch (FRPL). Low-poverty schools are those in which up to 25% are FRPL-eligible.

As I made mention in my video blog not too long ago, everything that is wrong in our society goes back to race. From the wealth disparity to segregation to the School to Prison pipeline, it all can be traced back I some way back to race. Now I realize that I greatly over simplified this, but you can at least understand how they all interconnected. And we have one group of individuals, who are so full of hate and vitriol towards minorities that they are willing to engage in armed rebellion against the United States, in order to achieve what they believe to be a purely a "white" nation. It is amazing how Trump not only condones these types of behavior, but encourages them through his rhetoric. By attempting to scare white suburban housewives to alluding to the fact that low-income (read: Blacks and Hispanics) housing is coming to the suburbs, bringing with them all the drugs and crime that goes along with that type of housing. But nothing could be further from the truth, and if they believe that rhetoric, then perhaps they are not as informed as we would like to think they are.

Now, remember when I mentioned that racial segregation? Ponder this for a moment, school segregation really lies at the epicenter of racial inequity in this country. Students in schools that are segregated by race and poverty have a much harder time graduating from high school and going to college, which makes it harder to get a job and to earn an income that allows them to support themselves and their family.

School segregation also feeds into housing segregation, which is a major source of the racial wealth gap. So, in order to deal with racial inequity, we have to address segregation. It's clear to me that this administration has no interest in this issue. You know, it's probably hostile to this issue. We have a secretary of education who does not value public education, clearly. So, let's just start there. Let's have somebody who is the secretary of education who values public education.

The current administration has no interest in this issue as far as I can tell. I don't even believe that the secretary of education values public education. But there are important things that the federal government could do. For example, it can provide financial support and technical expertise for school districts that want to integrate. Why should the public help in this fight to integrate public schools, and how would it benefit future generations?

We are living in a time of intense social divides
and racial "othering" that is often made worse by
social media. Other than K-12 public schools
and post-secondary education, it's hard for me
to think of a single place that provides sustained
opportunities for dynamic social interactions
with people from different backgrounds, where
people have the chance to relate to one another
across their differences.

When you engage with people across time, and
up close, you see their complexity. It's much
harder to stereotype and to make assumptions
about how "those people" are. Imagine if we
could replicate those experiences across public
schools? And there lies the rub, by learning
more about people, we run the risk of ending
any pre-conceived notions and beliefs about
them. I remember that while I was in college, I
had numerous interactions with various
minority groups, mostly positive, a very few
negative, and some just average human
interactions. What I have learned is they are just
like every other person, just trying to get by day
by day.

I'm not saying that it's easy; integration is hard
work. But it would move our country to a better
place if more people were open to difference and
didn't fear it.

Chapter Fifteen

We are going to close this book out with an examination of a school district who decided to do their school segregation correctly. I am talking about the Commonwealth of Kentucky's largest school district; Jefferson County.

Tracy E. K'Meyer, author of "From Brown to Meredith: The Long Struggle for School Desegregation in Louisville, Kentucky, 1954-2007," spent several years gathering the verbal narratives and history leading up to and through the desegregation of schools in Louisville.

"In 1964, when the civil rights act passed, it included a measure that said if your schools aren't integrated by 1974, you lose your federal funding," K'Meyer said.

Louisville's city and county schools were segregated at the time and as different as black and white. "About (1971) they got to Jefferson County," K'Meyer said. "They got to Jefferson County and found persistent segregation in Jefferson County Schools. The Kentucky Civil Liberties Union, the NAACP and the Kentucky Commission on Human Rights filed a lawsuit asking for the merger of the school systems and the desegregation of the systems." K'Meyer recently detailed the story of a teacher who thought someone was playing a joke on her when she arrived at her west-end school only to find out there was only one pair of scissors, and the teachers had to share them. "The classrooms didn't have scissors, and the teacher had to go down to the office to check out a pair of scissors for a couple of hours," K'Meyer said.

Pamela Smith was a student at Shawnee High School until her family moved to Shively. Although she loved Shawnee, she said she was surprised by the huge disparities between the school she attended in the west end and the school she attended after she moved. "We would read about science experiments and what was supposed to happen," she said. "We didn't actually get to see it because we didn't have working Bunsen burners or chemicals to do experiments with. We had to get the same information without the same resources."

In 1975, the appeals and arguments in the courtroom ceased and the drama moved to the classroom, and while the merger was good news for some people, there were opponents throughout the city. Edith Nelson Yarbrough was ready to attend high school but wasn't aware her life and the city around her were about to go through drastic changes.

"Late summer, we got a letter in the mail and the letter told me my assignment," she said, describing her reaction to the letter. "Wow. I'm going to Fairdale. Where is that? Where's Fairdale?" The school bus rides were long and in the first few weeks very dangerous. Under the court order, school enrollments had to be between 15 and 50 percent black. White students were bused for two of their 12 years of schooling. black students as many as 10. Then-Gov. Julian Carroll called on the Kentucky National Guard during the first few days of forced busing to protect the students and the buses.

"As that bus slowed down into the parking lot, we had sticks, cans, bricks, limbs of trees all thrown at the bus," Lynn Elliot told WAVE 3 News as tears streamed down here face. "A lot of us were on the floor of the bus." Elliot added that she was horrified, but what was worse than having thing thrown at her and her friends was what was said to them. "I can remember finding something that said a n***** hunting license, and it talked about what you could do to a black person," she said. "I don't think that one could ever be prepared for what we went through."

John Stovall, who now works for JCPS, was a student who lived in Fern Creek. Stovall was bused from his home school Moore to Thomas Jefferson. "I remember them burning tires in front of Southern High School," he said. "I remember the KKK." Stovall said the kids handled the conflict better than the adults did. "Back in the day, this side of town had this, and this side of town had that, and you really didn't intermingle," he said.

No one likes to be told what to do, especially to change something that has benefitted them for almost 350 years at that time. If left to their own devices, segregation would still be the norm within the United States, and we would truly have such a thing as white privilege. So it stands to reason that people would offer up resistance to something new, especially if that something new meant that their whole way of thinking has been challenged. And I believe, and this opinion is mine and mine alone, but one of the major points of contention to desegregation is the fact that the children's belief and value system is being challenged without parental bias. And without that parental bias, the child is free to develop their own opinions regarding race and members of different minority groups.

In 2017, the Kentucky GOP-led state House had just passed a bill that requiring Jefferson County to return to neighborhood schooling, undoing the county's longstanding desegregation efforts. It was defeated in the Kentucky Senate.

During the Democratic Presidential Primary Debates, Kamala Harris and Joe Biden have catapulted a long-running debate about "busing" and school integration back into the news. Harris' criticism of fellow Democratic presidential candidate Biden for his vigorous opposition to court-ordered desegregation in the 1970s has also sparked fresh debate about whether those efforts were successful.

What do we know? In the most basic sense, they did succeed. School segregation dropped substantially as courts and the federal government put pressure on local districts to integrate. But those efforts also sparked bitter, sometimes racist, resistance that shaped political discourse for decades.

"Busing as a political term ... was a failure, because the narrative that came out of it from the media and politicians was almost only negative," said Matt Delmont, a Dartmouth historian who wrote a book titled "Why Busing Failed." "It only emphasized the inconvenience to white families and white students."

A political failure does not necessarily mean an educational failure, though, as Delmont and others have pointed out. Indeed, research has consistently shown that integrated schools offered, and still offer, tangible benefits to students of color. Since public schools in many places today remain intensely segregated by race and socioeconomic status, this issue is not just a historical one. "School integration didn't fail," Berkeley economist Rucker Johnson, who has conducted some of the most far-reaching research on school integration, recently argued. "The only failure is that we stopped pursuing it and allowed the reign of segregation to return."

At the same time, there is evidence that desegregation efforts have had some unintended consequences, like the loss of black teachers.

Here's what research tells us about how these desegregation policies worked. Research shows that school desegregation, often including "busing," helped black students in the long run. To isolate the impact of court-ordered school integration in the 1960s, '70s, and '80s, Johnson used two strategies. First, he compared students in the same school district right before and after court-ordered integration was put in place. Second, he compared pairs of siblings, when one went to integrated schools but the other didn't.

His conclusions were similar: integration helped black students academically and into adulthood. The effects were quite large: going to integrated schools for an additional five years caused high school graduation rates to jump by nearly 15 percentage points and reduced the likelihood of living in poverty by 11 percentage points. In a follow-up analysis, Johnson found that these benefits extended to the next generation. The children of those who attended integrated schools had higher test scores and were more likely to attend college, too.

Johnson's work is consistent with other research. Another national paper found that school desegregation efforts in the '70s reduced the dropout rate among black students, though the effect was smaller than Johnson's estimate. A study focusing on Louisiana between 1965 and 1970 found that integration dramatically boosted black students' chances of graduating high school. Why did school integration make such a difference? Johnson and others show that black students ended up attending much better resourced schools with smaller class sizes. "Court-ordered desegregation that led to larger improvements in school quality resulted in more beneficial educational, economic, and health outcomes in adulthood for blacks who grew up in those court-ordered desegregation districts," Johnson concludes.

More recent research continues to find benefits of integrated schools, though they tend to be somewhat smaller. One study found that when desegregation orders were lifted between 1991 and 2010 in many districts, essentially the reverse of what Johnson looked at, dropout rates jumped by 3 percentage points among Hispanic students and 1 point among black students. "If policymakers have an interest in increasing the graduation rate of black and Hispanic youth, one tool in their disposal, is promoting racially integrated schools," said researcher David Liebowitz. A separate study of an anonymous city school district found that scrapping race-based integration efforts in the early 2000s reduced college enrollment among black students.

. Louisville was the first major metropolitan area to implement a court-ordered busing plan to desegregate its city and county schools all at once, and in the four decades since the federal government first told Louisville to integrate its schools, the city has done so with an unrivaled commitment. Its desegregation efforts eventually became broadly popular among students, teachers, administrators and parents, white and black alike, and Louisville has kept at them, even as many other cities and federal policymakers — many current Democratic presidential candidates included — have abandoned the cause.

If you really want to understand the fight over desegregating public schools, you should take a look at the place that's still committed to doing it.

Desegregation wasn't popular when it arrived in Louisville. Forty-four years ago, a federal judge ruled that the city had failed to comply with Brown v. Board of Education — the landmark 1954 case in which the Supreme Court ruled that separate-but-equal schooling violated the Constitution — and ordered it to desegregate its schools. The ruling forced the merger of city and county schools into a single district, called Jefferson County Public Schools, and instituted racial quotas for student populations.

Six weeks later, on the second day of the school year, thousands of angry white students walked out of their classrooms and rioted. They torched school buses and chucked rocks at the police, who had been dispatched to help enforce the court ruling. Protests took place especially in the south end of the city, where largely white, working-class schools took in black students, some of them for the first time.

It was a typical scene for 1975, in the midst of a national effort, led by the U.S. Department of Education, the Supreme Court and the federal courts below it, to desegregate America's schools.

Images like those from Louisville remain seared in the national conscience when it comes to those debates and help inform why so many seem to regard "busing" as a cosmic and total failure of American policymaking.

But it's what happened next, in the weeks and years and decades after those protests died down, that should inform those debates instead.

By the end of the first week, the majority of residents in Louisville seemed "overwhelmingly to be accepting, quietly if grudgingly, the busing of 11,300 black students from the city to the suburbs and of 11,300 white students — out of a total of 118,000 students of both races, in the opposite direction," The New York Times reported at the time.

Eventually, the National Guardsmen who had tried to help ensure smooth implementation of the busing program moved on to other causes, and, although some white Louisvillians fled the public-school system for the surrounding counties or enrolled their children in all-white parochial and private schools, the city largely moved ahead with the busing program.

And that experience still helps explain the program's success and why Louisville has continued its efforts to desegregate even without the federal oversight that once compelled it to.

When the national political mood was becoming inhospitable to school desegregation plans...in Louisville and Jefferson County a biracial integrationist coalition and eventually the school board itself fought to protect diversity in the local schools.

Critiques of desegregation policies often focus on their effects on academic achievement, and on that front, districts like JCPS have acquitted themselves well: "The peak years of desegregation" saw "mixed test score results but a positive trend toward higher African American student achievement," as well as "long-term academic and professional gains for African American adults who had attended racially mixed schools," one review of school desegregation studies found. Other studies have suggested that students from all races make achievement gains when they attend diverse schools.

And, although racial and ethnic achievement gaps still persist, research has shown that the gulf between black and white students is smaller in integrated schools. Black and Latino students who attend integrated schools also score higher on college entrance exams like the SAT, studies have suggested, and students in such schools are less likely to drop out and more likely to go to college than those who attend heavily segregated schools. White students, meanwhile, show no real change in pure educational achievement at integrated schools, so, although busing is often viewed by white parents as a zero-sum affair, the data suggests the downsides are virtually nonexistent. School integration is beneficial to black and white students who experience it alike.

Teachers, administrators and white and minority parents and students in Jefferson County tend to agree, according to a 2011 survey. And more comprehensive research has found that students who attend desegregated schools "benefit from access to integrated social networks and positive interactions with students of different races and ethnicities, and are more likely to live and work in integrated environments upon reaching adulthood." It is said to reduce racial bias and prejudice, especially among whites.

"Forced busing," in other words, has had profound effects on the city as a whole and the people who live there, and almost immediately the Louisvillians who'd experienced it under the first iteration of desegregation became its biggest champions — white students who were bused were later among those who started a nonprofit group that advocated for school integration. Which may be why Louisville hasn't given up on school desegregation efforts even when the federal government has given it a chance to.

In the 1980s and then again in the 1990s, Jefferson County Public Schools, believing it had satisfied the federal requirements, attempted to make major changes to its desegregation policies in ways that many in the community feared would result in the re-segregation of its schools. But each attempt was met instead by broad and racially diverse coalitions of activists and organizations who "stood up for preserving integration and diversity in the schools," as University of Louisville history professor Tracy E. K'Meyer has observed. "As a result, the school board over time altered but did not end the busing plan."

So, during a period "when the national political mood was becoming inhospitable to school desegregation plans," K'Meyer wrote in her book about desegregation in the city, "in Louisville and Jefferson County a biracial integrationist coalition and eventually the school board itself fought to protect diversity in the local schools."

And instead of dramatic overhauls, JCPS constantly tweaked its approach to desegregation, giving parents slightly more choice in where their children went to school, attempting to reduce the inequitable burden busing placed on black students, reintegrating some aspects of neighborhood schooling and implementing magnet programs across the city to make schools more attractive, all while maintaining desegregation as an overarching goal of how it assigned students to various schools.

I found this very interesting. When other southern metropolitan school districts were fighting tooth and nail to keep desegregation from happening in their schools, Louisville and Jefferson County schools after initial resistance, accepted desegregation and made every effort to make a very complex issue work for the maximum number of students. Of course, Louisville, during the Antebellum period, had a very large slave market there, and it was customary for slaveholders to sell "troublesome" slaves to plantations further down south, where their conditions were a lot worse. This is where we get the saying, "Sold down the river."

Then, in 2007, the U.S. Supreme Court invalidated the quota-based busing plan Jefferson County Public Schools had used to desegregate, giving forced integration skeptics yet another opening and the district an out. For the last decade, conservatives and well-funded education "reform" groups have pushed various policies that, whether by design or by accident, have rolled back a half-century of progress across the country, and today, many of the nation's public school districts are as segregated, and in some cases even more segregated, than they were when Brown v. Board of Education was handed down in 1954.

But Louisville and JCPS have remained committed to desegregation. School officials there responded to the Supreme Court decision by implementing a new student assignment plan meant to comply with the law but achieve the same ends: Instead of relying solely on race, it incorporated socio-economic and poverty statistics into its plans, too.

It was, by and large, successful, and that persistence has earned Louisville plaudits as "the city that believed in desegregation" and made Jefferson County Public Schools, as Penn State education researcher Erica Frankenberg told me last year, "a real national model for commitment" to integration.

However, this success is NOT without its detractors. A recent survey commissioned by the district showed dwindling support for the plan and a decreased interest in diversity among parents. Struggling schools and a yawning achievement gap between black and white students are drawing more attention these days than the benefits of maintaining racially integrated classrooms.

As the district's schools slowly become more segregated, officials are considering more reforms that will almost certainly increase segregation.

The state's Department of Education proposed taking over the district last year after finding myriad problems, from financial mismanagement to flaws in the desegregation program, known as the student assignment plan. State officials agreed to give district leaders until next year to carry out reforms.

"Right now, we're doing our best to fight back Jim Crow and Jane Crow Jr.," said Delquan Dorsey, Ms. Lewis's son, who works as the district's community engagement coordinator. "We know separate but equal doesn't work."

There are dozens of school districts across the country like Louisville that continue to follow desegregation plans, whether court ordered or not, with supporters often pointing to research that suggests the black-white achievement gap narrows where integration is fully accepted. And yet opposition has never been very far behind.

In the past two decades, dozens of affluent, mostly white communities have tried to secede from diverse school districts to form their own. A conservative law firm filed a lawsuit last year to challenge a decades-old system that helped desegregate public schools in Hartford. A current lawsuit in Minnesota argues that the state's school system is unconstitutionally segregated.

Louisville's integration program has existed since the 1975 court order merged city schools with suburban ones. The year before, a similar plan in Detroit was struck down by the United States Supreme Court.

Both Louisville and Detroit were about 20 percent black and equally racially segregated at the time, according to a report by Myron Orfield Jr., the director of the Institute on Metropolitan Opportunity at the University of Minnesota. But in the decades that followed, Detroit's schools became overwhelmingly black and underperforming as white residents fled for suburban enclaves.

Louisville is now part of a countywide school system of roughly 100,000 students that is 42 percent white, 37 percent black and 12 percent Hispanic. About half of its black students, and two-thirds of all students, attend integrated schools, according to Will Stancil, a research fellow at the institute who defined integrated as having a population between 20 percent and 60 percent nonwhite.

By 2011, black students in Louisville were twice as likely to score "proficient" on math and reading tests as those in Detroit, Mr. Orfield found.

Despite the protests that occurred in the immediate aftermath of bussing's implementation, it seems that forced integration fostered support among Louisvillians for it, especially as a generation that went to integrated schools became parents who wanted their children to learn in integrated spaces, too.

In 1975, as many as 90% of local residents, and 98% of white parents — opposed the plan. A

2011 poll, however, found that 89% of parents who had children in Jefferson County Public Schools supported desegregation in theory, and surveys of students themselves found broad support as well. The same survey suggested that residents' commitment to desegregation was more than philosophical, as nearly half of white parents said they'd support desegregation policies even if it meant their own child had to cross neighborhoods to attend school.

It's possible such polls overstate the popularity of specific desegregation policies, but Louisvillians have consistently shown support for the city's actual plans at the ballot box: School board candidates who have run against the district's student-assignment plan have faced overwhelming defeats even in the wake of the 2007 Supreme Court ruling, according to The Atlantic.

In the years since, opaque organizations with nondescript names have poured hundreds of thousands of dollars into school board races to no avail. Two years ago, a Republican-backed "neighborhood schools plan" that would have effectively ended Jefferson County's desegregation efforts stalled amid vocal opposition. And last year, a proposed state takeover of JCPS that threatened the district's aggressive desegregation efforts drew widespread opposition in Louisville, in part because locals saw it as an effort to "effectively re-segregate our schools," as Chris Brady, a member of the

Jefferson County Board of Education, told me at the time.

That's not to say Jefferson County is perfect or that it doesn't need to make substantial progress to achieve equality and improve its schools. Too many of its students, especially those in black neighborhoods, still attend schools with high concentrations of poverty, and its low-income schools — which are largely located in the overwhelmingly black neighborhoods west of the city — remain far behind in terms of equity and achievement. Its efforts at desegregation might not be ambitious enough, in practical or idealistic terms. And inside school, white kids like me were and still are more likely to wind up in Advanced Placement classes, meaning there were still pockets of segregation even in a broadly desegregated space — a problem many integrated schools haven't adequately addressed. Students of color are more likely to be suspended. And, though most black Louisvillians support desegregation efforts, there has long been concern that the district's efforts still place an unequal burden on black children. The list goes on and on.

Parents and community leaders in the suburbs fought the plan vociferously, and when the case reached the Supreme Court, in 1974, the majority called the integration plan "wholly impermissible." In its Milliken decision, the Court threw out the idea that suburban districts in the Detroit area had to be part of the city school district. The suburbs had not participated in discrimination, Justice Burger wrote in his opinion, and should not be punished. Desegregation does not require "any particular racial balance in each 'school, grade or classroom,'" he wrote.

The decision led to even more segregation in Detroit, as white families continued to move to the suburbs, in large part to put their kids in the schools there, bringing with them tax revenue and businesses. By 2006, the city of Detroit's public schools were 91 percent black and 3 percent white, while the schools in the district of Grosse Pointe, which borders Detroit, were about 89 percent white and 8 percent black.

"One of the reasons white people leave central cities is because schools become segregated before neighborhoods do," Orfield said. "White families stop buying in certain areas where the schools become all poor and non-white."

Now the city of Detroit is 83 percent black, while Oakland County, north of the city, is 78 percent white, and is the richest county in the state. In Detroit, 39 percent of people were below the poverty line in 2009-2013, according to Census data, while just 10 percent of Oakland County was.

Detroit wasn't the only place that successfully fought a metropolitan-wide school integration plan. Richmond, Virginia, avoided a similar plan in the 1970s, leading to widespread segregation in county and city schools. In fact, a number of cities in the north and east have avoided metropolitan-wide plans and created a system of mostly black city public schools and white suburban public schools, according to Erika Frankenberg, a Penn State professor who studies the issue.

This is what makes Louisville so unusual. Even after the Milliken decision, a panel in December of 1974 ordered the integration of the city and county schools to continue in the region. Beginning in 1975, students were sorted alphabetically and bused to different schools around the county. Under the order, schools in the county had to be between 15 and 50 percent black.

The Louisville plan wasn't popular at first. Thousands of protesters rallied against busing at the district's schools, protesting and vandalizing police cars until the governor called in the Kentucky National Guard to supervise buses for the first few days.

But something strange happened as the integration plan continued. Many of the residents' fears failed to materialize, and after a few years the protests ceased.

It's as though "people are amazed to discover that people from another race or ethnic group are actually pretty similar to them," said Gary Orfield, the co-director of the Civil Rights Project at UCLA, who has worked with the city for decades on the plan (and is Myron Orfield's brother). "There's a tremendous deflation of protests when almost all the stereotypes people hold aren't true."

Orfield remembers the vitriol in Louisville in 1975, when the unions and white population alike vehemently protested the court order—at one point, a bishop supportive of the integration was spat on as he came out of church. But Orfield also remembers how, five years after the plan began and the judge ceased active supervision of the court order, the region's leaders "decided what he had done was a good idea and they had a banquet for him." Not everyone felt this way—Jefferson County saw a drop-off in enrollment after the integration, but it later leveled off.

Much has changed in the decades since the bussing plan began. Surveys done back in the 1970s indicated that 98 percent of suburban residents opposed the plan. But in a 2011 survey, 89 percent of parents in Jefferson County said they thought that the school district's guidelines should "ensure that students learn with students from different races and economic backgrounds." About 87 percent of parents asked said they were satisfied with the quality of their child's education.

By 2006, after a frustrated parent fought the busing plan all the way to the Supreme Court, many in Louisville preferred integration to the alternative. The case was named for Crystal Meredith, who had moved to Louisville in 2002 and was required to send her son to a school 10 miles away since the school near her home was full. She and other parents argued that the plan violated their children's Fourteenth Amendment right to equal protection under the law. Their case was merged with Parents Involved, a similar case from Seattle.

When a bitterly divided Supreme Court struck down Jefferson County's integration plan, students and parents spoke openly about how they disagreed with the decision. One graduate of Jefferson County Public Schools wrote an impassioned op-ed in the local paper, suggesting that among those who opposed integration, there was "no talk of society as a collective group, no concern for others, no consideration of communal benefit." He recounted an experience he'd had at college in Virginia, where peers chanted racist slogans and carried around Confederate flags during an "Old South" fraternity party—a display that horrified him, he said, in part because he had been exposed to diversity in Louisville.

In a sign of how much the region had changed since the 1970s, the district pledged to maintain its commitment to diversity even after the Supreme Court ruling. "This community really values an integrated school system. It is a core value within Jefferson County," superintendent

Sheldon Berman told the Louisville Courier-Journal in reaction to the decision. "We will find some creative ways to continue to model that."

Their initial plan used household income and a complex busing system to try and integrate students, but it confused parents and was not very effective. So Jefferson County brought in Gary Orfield and asked him to help design a plan that would follow the law but still keep the district's schools diverse.

Currently, the district puts schools in "clusters," which are groups of diverse neighborhoods. Parents fill out an application listing their preferences for certain schools in the cluster, and the district assigns students to certain schools in order to achieve diversity goals. It does this by ranking census blocks on a number of factors, including the percentage minority residents, the educational attainment of adults, and household income, and mixing up students from various blocks. Parents can appeal the school assignments, but have no guarantee of getting their top choice. They can also apply for magnet schools and special programs such as Spanish-language immersion.

Parents who went through Jefferson County Public Schools themselves tend to especially appreciate the system's diversity. Jessica Goldstein was a first grader in 1977, and vaguely remembers crowds of people standing around the school on her first few days in protest. Goldstein, who is white, says some of her friends avoided being bused by filing for medical exemptions, saying allergies, headaches, and other health concerns would make busing a hardship. But Goldstein was bused, starting in middle school, to a school in Louisville's predominantly black West End.

"I remember very clearly my mother telling me that I shouldn't even think about trying to get out of it," she told me. "That she went to school when they were completely segregated by race and that it was wrong. No complaining, no nagging, no asking questions and I was going to get on the bus and I was going to go."

Goldstein actually liked the school in the black neighborhood more than the one she'd been attending in her predominantly white neighborhood. She filed a petition to continue to attend that school (this was needed since, at the time, white students were only bused for two of their first 12 years of schooling, in contrast with black students were bused for up to 10) and it was granted. "I think it was very beneficial to go to school and to be friends with and spend your day with people whose economic conditions and life stories are very different from yours," Goldstein reflected. "It instilled an attitude of gratitude; it helped build some perspective."

In fact, over the years, studies have shown that students who attended the integrated schools in Jefferson County were better prepared to work with people from different racial or ethnic backgrounds and held fewer stereotypes than those who did not attend integrated schools.

"One of the reasons white people leave central cities is because schools become segregated before neighborhoods do."

City-county school integration also reduced white flight from the city of Louisville, keeping home values and tax revenues stable, says Genevieve Siegel-Hawley, who conducted a study comparing housing segregation in four cities that had different school-integration policies.

When parents decide to buy a home, they often make choices based on neighborhood schools. This has an effect on home prices: One Connecticut study found that buyers were willing to pay $7,468 more for a house near a less diverse school. But parents in Louisville know that whether they buy a house in the city or the suburbs, their child will go to a school that has similar resources—and racial breakdown—as other schools in the district.

"When families are thinking about moving around the metro area, they know that any neighborhood is going to be linked to a school with a racial composition that reflects the broader-metropolitan area," she said. "It helps disentangle the school-housing relationship."

In fact, the rate of segregation in Louisville's housing declined more quickly than in other cities after the school-integration plan, falling more than 20 percent between 1990 and 2010. That rate of the decline in housing segregation was double that of the Richmond area, which had avoided city-county school integration.

"This central finding suggests that, in some ways, school policy can become housing policy," Siegel-Hawley concluded, in the study.

It helped that Louisville was also one of the few metropolitan areas that made a concerted effort to integrate housing as it integrated the schools, Siegel-Hawley said. Some African American families received vouchers to move to white areas of town and were exempt from busing. Neighborhoods that were racially balanced would sometimes be exempted from busing. One human rights group even posted billboards around town that read "Fight Forced Busing, Support Fair Housing" to remind people that more integrated neighborhood would mean fewer bus rides for students.

The city-county school integration has also led to a more-solid tax base in Louisville, since families aren't leaving the city. Louisville's tax base was 122 percent of the regional average in 2008, Orfield said, and its bond rating was Aa2, or high quality, in 2010. In Detroit, where residents fled to the suburbs in part because of schools, the tax base was 28 percent of the regional average and in 2012 its bond rating was junk status, Orfield found.

A survey JCPS conducted last year suggested that the overall plan isn't popular: Just 20% of Louisville parents believe the current method of assigning children to schools is working, and the numbers are even worse among black parents. Just 40% of white Louisvillians, meanwhile, expressed "high agreement" with the idea that the district's guidelines should "ensure diversity" among its student bodies. But dig deeper, and the chief concern with the plan is its ability to get children into quality schools — a broader problem JCPS needs to address — rather than its focus on desegregation. Among students, parents and Louisvillians generally, the survey found that less than 10% disagreed with "using enrollment guidelines to ensure that students learn alongside peers from races and backgrounds other than their own."

School officials in Jefferson County have, at least publicly, taken those shortcomings seriously, launching new policies aimed at addressing existing iniquities. And amid threats of a state takeover last year, they promised to re-evaluate, and possibly overhaul, its current processes for assigning students to schools — a move that will keep the reform process in the hands of local officials who see desegregation as a priority. And whatever changes occur, it seems clear, a half-century after the federal government forced it to start desegregating its schools through busing, that Louisville remains committed to building on that foundation and keeping its schools from re-segregating.

Critics say an integrated learning environment is not enough, especially when black students continue to lag behind their white peers, and often shoulder a greater burden in desegregation, with longer bus rides.

There, at least, the question is one of how rather than if. But how Jefferson County reached that point still matters historically. "I think of busing as being in the toolbox of what is available and what can be used for the goal of desegregating America's schools," Harris said days after the debate in what some viewed as an effort to walk back her criticism of Biden. "I believe that any tool that is in the toolbox should be considered by a school district."

Busing was in the toolbox in Louisville. But only because the federal government put it there.

Conclusion

There you have it, we as a country in the 1960's (1964 to be exact, the year of my birth,) set forth on fully realizing what the founding fathers set forth when they decided to create that "more perfect union," with the foundation of that union being "that all men are created equal, endowed with their creator with certain inalienable rights, those being life, liberty, and the pursuit of happiness." Of course, these were the same founding fathers who decided that Blacks would count as 3/5th of a person when it came Census time. But it was a noble goal, none the less.

Have we really progressed much from either 1789 or 1873 (the year Reconstruction ended in the South?) I really don't think so. Ever since the end of the Civil War, we have had people who have terrorized Blacks and as more minorities came to this country, the larger their basis for hatred became. Eventually, the Ku Klux Klan came to hate not only Blacks, but Jews, Catholics, Hispanics and people of Oriental descent. They aren't the first hate group in the United States, for that you have to go back to the 1840's and the "Know-Nothings," which were an actual political party / domestic terror group, which actually manage to elect a Governor of Kentucky, but they fizzled out about the same time the Whigs did.

Now you have all kinds of hate groups operating within the United States, each spouting their own type of vitriol. But probably the most dangerous hate group out there doesn't even know they are a hate group. I'm talking about the white suburbanite voter. Before you judge, hear me out, because I, like you, are either one or was raised in one.

A suburbanite of today is pretty much like the suburbanite of years gone by. Conservative, had a small circle of friends, attends church. But the major difference is now both parents have to work to maintain a middle-class lifestyle. And parents have become more over-protective, hence the term, "helicopter parents." They are the ones who fear change the most. They want their children to go to the best schools academically, and will fight till their dying breath against any type of change that could possibly lower their children's school's academic reputation. That is the main reason for the opposition to integration. Instead of having the expectation that the minority students can rise to the academic expectations, they fear that they will lower it, which is in and of itself, a prejudicial statement. The next time a middle-class white suburbanite says that they are not prejudiced, just pose the question to them of whether or not they would be comfortable having minority students attend the sane school as their children. And then watch them squirm and make all kinds of excuses for **not** wanting their school integrated.

The truth is, the suburbs are full of minorities, Black, Hispanic, Muslim, Hindu, Chinese, Japanese, whatever. This phenomenon is more prevalent than people want to believe. So much for the suburbs being the last bastion of whiteness. Now if you want to find affluent white people, you go to the city. The city, where gentrification has caused a major shift in socio-economics, but also a refocus on race and race relations. As gentrification takes place, areas that used to be the "bad side" of town are exactly where young people yearn to be. Old building are remodeled into apartments or condominiums, nice restaurants, coffee shops and boutiques move into what was vacant storefronts, and all is well. But those displaced have to go somewhere, right? Ponder on that. Take all the time you need.

Will we ever achieve equality in our educational institutions? I am not going to say whether we will or will not. But if we are to do so, we are going to have to change our attitudes towards both race and education. Given our current mindset and race relations in this country, I would not hold my breath on seeing any attitude changes in regards to education and race.

Works Cited

"BROWN V. BOARD: Timeline of School Integration in the U.S". April 2004.

Reardon, Sean F.; Owens, Ann (2014). "60 Years After Brown: Trends and Consequences of School Segregation". Annual Review of Sociology. 40 (1): 199–218. doi:10.1146/annurev-soc-071913-043152. ISSN 0360-0572.

Reardon, Sean F. (2016). "School Segregation and Racial Academic Achievement Gaps". RSF: The Russell Sage Foundation Journal of the Social Sciences. 2 (5): 34–57. doi:10.7758/RSF.2016.2.5.03. ISSN 2377-8253.

"Racial Segregation in the American South: Jim Crow Laws." Prejudice in the Modern World Reference Library. Ed. Kelly Rudd, Richard Hanes, and Sarah Hermsen. Vol. 2. Detroit: UXL, 2007. 333-357. Global Issues in Context. Web. 19 Oct. 2013.

"Jim Crow Laws". National Park Service. Retrieved November 1, 2013.

Powers, Jeanne M.; Patton, Lirio (March 1, 2008). "Between Mendez and Brown: Gonzales v. Sheely (1951) and the Legal Campaign Against Segregation". Law & Social Inquiry. 33 (1): 127–171. doi:10.1111/j.1747-4469.2008.00096.x. ISSN 1747-4469.

Donato, Ruben; Guzmán, Gonzalo; Hanson, Jarrod (2017). "Francisco Maestas et al. v. George H. Shone et al: Mexican American Resistance to School Segregation in the Hispano Homeland, 1912–1914". Journal of Latinos and Education. 16 (1): 3–17. doi:10.1080/15348431.2016.1179190.

Donato, Rubén; Hanson, Jarrod (June 15, 2012). "Legally White, Socially "Mexican": The Politics of De Jure and De Facto School Segregation in the American Southwest". Harvard Educational Review. 82 (2): 202–225. doi:10.17763/haer.82.2.a562315u72355106.

Foley, Nick (2010). Quest for Equality: The Failed Promise of Black-Brown Solidarity. Cambridge, MA: Harvard University Press. ISBN 9780674050235.

Orfield, Gary. "Schools More Separate: Consequences of a Decade of Resegregation." Harvard Civil Rights Project. (2001). (accessed September 24, 2013)

Sean Reardon; Anne Owens (October 2013). "60 Years After Brown: Trends and Consequences of School Segregation" (PDF). Stanford University.

Powers, Jeanne M. (November 1, 2014). "On Separate Paths: The Mexican American and African American Legal Campaigns against School Segregation". American Journal of Education. 121 (1): 29–55. doi:10.1086/678124. ISSN 0195-6744.

Kluger, Richard (2004). Simple Justice: The History of Brown v. Board of Education and Black America's Struggle for Equality. New York: Vintage. ISBN 978-1400030613.

"Cardinal Joseph E. Ritter". Marian University. Archived from the original on May 27, 2010. Retrieved January 22, 2019.

"Most Rev. William Adrian, Ex-Bishop of Tennessee". The New York Times. February 15, 1972.

Paretsky, Sara (2007). Writing in an Age of Silence. Verso. pp. 49.

Stroub, Kori J., and Meredith P. Richards. "From Resegregation to Reintegration: Trends in the Racial/Ethnic Segregation of Metropolitan Public School." American Educational Research Journal. no. 3 (2013): 497-531. (accessed September 24, 2013)

Fiel, Jeremy E. "Decomposing School Resegregation: Social Closure, Racial Imbalance, and Racial Isolation." American Sociological Review. no. 5 (20 13): 1-21. (accessed September 24, 2013)

Frankenberg, Erica. Frankenberg, Erica (2013). "The Role of Residential Segregation in Contemporary School Segregation". Education and Urban Society. 45 (5): 548–570. doi:10.1177/0013124513486288.

Reardon, Sean; John Yun (2002). "Integrating neighborhoods, segregating schools: The retreat from school desegregation in the South, 1990-2000" (PDF). North Carolina Law Review. 81. Retrieved October 19, 2013.

Chemerinsky, Erwin. "The Segregation and Resegregation of American Public Education: The Court's Role." North Carolina Law Review. (2003): 1598-1622. (accessed September 24, 2013).

Dorsey, Dana N. "Segregation 2.0: The New Generation of School Segregation in the 21st Century." Education and Urban Society. no. 5 (2013). (accessed September 24, 2013)

Reardon, Sean F., Elena T. Grewal, Demetra Kalogrides, and Erica Greenberg. "Brown Fades: The End of Court-Ordered School Desegregation and the Resegregation of American Public Schools." Journal of Policy Analysis and Management. no. 4 (2012): 876-904. (accessed September 24, 2013)

Tefera, Adai; Erica Frankenberg; Genevieve Siegel-Hawley; Gina Chirichigno (2011). "Integrating Suburban Schools: How to Benefit from Growing Diversity and Avoid Segregation" (PDF). UCLA Civil Right Project. Retrieved October 19, 2013.

Frankenberg, Erica; Genevieve Siegel-Hawley (November 2009). "Equity Overlooked: Charter

Schools and Civil Rights Policy" (PDF). The Civil Rights Project. Retrieved November 4, 2013.

Miron, G., Urschel, J. L., Mathis, W, J., & Tornquist, E. "Schools without Diversity: Education Management Organizations, Charter Schools and the Demographic Stratification of the American School System" (2010). Boulder and Tempe: Education and the Public Interest Center & Education Policy Research Unit. (accessed September 24, 2013)

Orfield, Gary; John Kucsera; Genevieve Siegel-Hawley (September 2012). "E Pluribus...Separation: Deepening Double Segregation for More Students" (PDF). The Civil Rights Project. Retrieved November 1, 2013.

Hanushek, Eric A.; John F. Kain; Steven G. Rivkin (2009). "New Evidence about Brown v. Board of Education: The Complex Effects of School Racial Composition on Achievement" (PDF). Journal of Labor Economics. 27 (3): 349–383. doi:10.1086/600386. JSTOR 10.1086/600386.

Mickelson, Roslyn Arlin; Mokubung Nkomo (March 2012). "Integrated Schooling, Life Course Outcomes, and Social Cohesion in Multiethnic Democratic Societies". Review of Research in Education. 36 (1): 197–238. doi:10.3102/0091732x11422667.

Hanushek, Eric A.; Finis Welch (2006). Has School Desegregation Improved Academic and

Economic Outcomes for Blacks? (PDF).
Handbook of the Economics of Education. 2. pp.
1019–1049. doi:10.1016/s1574-0692(06)02017-
4. ISBN 9780444528193. Retrieved November
19, 2013.

Wells, Amy Stuart; Robert L. Crain (1994).
"Perpetuation Theory and the Long-Term Effects
of School Desegregation". Review of Educational
Research. 64 (4): 531–555.
doi:10.3102/00346543064004531.

Reardon, Sean F.; John T. Yun; Michal
Kurlaender (2006). "Implications of Income-
Based School Assignment Policies for Racial
School Segregation". Educational Evaluation and
Policy Analysis. 28 (1): 49–75.
doi:10.3102/01623737028001049. JSTOR
3699542.

Kahlenberg, Richard D. (2012). "From All Walks
of Life: New Hope for School Integration" (PDF).
American Educator. Retrieved November 21,
2013.

Rumberger, Russell W.; Gregory J. Palardy
(2005). "Does Segregation Still Matter? The
Impact of Student Composition on Academic
Achievement in High School" (PDF). Teachers
College Record. 107 (9). Archived from the
original (PDF) on December 4, 2010. Retrieved
November 24, 2013.

Wells, Amy Stuart (2001). "The 'Consequences'
of School Desegregation: The Mismatch Between

the Research and the Rationale" (PDF). Hastings Constitutional Law Quarterly. 28. Retrieved November 19, 2013.